Katô Shidzue

Representatives Katô Kanjû and Katô Shidzue with their daughter
Taki at home, 1947. Courtesy of Katô Shidzue.

Helen M. Hopper
University of Pittsburgh

Katô Shidzue

A Japanese Feminist

The Library of World Biography

Series Editor: Peter N. Stearns

PEARSON
Longman

New York   San Francisco   Boston
London   Toronto   Sydney   Singapore   Madrid
Mexico City   Munich   Paris   Cape Town   Hong Kong   Montreal

Vice President and Publisher: Priscilla McGeehon
Acquisitions Editor: Erika Gutierrez
Executive Marketing Manager: Sue Westmoreland
Production Coordinator: Shafiena Ghani
Senior Cover Design Manager and Cover Designer: Nancy Danahy
Cover Photo: Baroness Shidzu Ihimoto, Town Hall Tea, November
    11, 1932. © Keystone-Underwood, New York, Margaret Sanger
    Papers. (*Note:* Margaret Sanger and Mrs. Ruth Lut have been
    cropped out of this picture.) Sophia Smith Collection, Smith
    College.
Text Designer: Alice Fernandes-Brown
Electronic Production Specialist: Jeff Streber
Manufacturing Buyer: Roy Pickering
Printer and Binder: R.R. Donnelley and Sons Company/Harrisonburg
Cover Printer: Coral Graphics Services, Inc.

Library of Congress Cataloging-in-Publication Data
Hopper, Helen M.
    Katô Shidzue: a Japanese feminist / Helen M. Hopper.
        p. cm. -- (Library of world biography)
    Includes bibliographical references and index.
    ISBN 0-321-07804-7
        1. Katô, Shidzue, 1897- 2. Feminists--Japan--Biography. 3.Women
    politicians--Japan--Biography. I. Title. II. Series.

HQ1762.5.K38 H66 2002
952.04'092--dc21
[B]   2002025486

Please visit our website at http://www.ablongman.com

ISBN 0–321–07804–7

For Ashino Yuriko

Contents

Editor's Preface

"Biography is history seen through the prism of a person."

—Louis Fischer

It is often challenging to identify the roles and experiences of individuals in world history. Larger forces predominate. Yet biography provides important access to world history. It shows how individuals helped shape the society around them. Biography also offers concrete illustrations of larger patterns, in political and intellectual life, in family life, and in the economy.

The Longman Library of World Biography series seeks to capture the individuality and drama that mark human character. It deals with individuals operating in one of the main periods of world history, while also reflecting issues in the particular society around them. Here, the individual illustrates larger themes of time and place. The interplay between the personal and the general is always the key to using biography in history, and world history is no exception. Always, too, there is the question of personal agency: how much do individuals, even great ones, shape their own lives and environment, and how much are they shaped by the world around them?

PETER STEARNS

Prologue

Katô Shidzue, who was born into an upper-class Tokyo family just before the turn of the twentieth century, was educated to become a traditional Japanese "good wife and wise mother." When, at seventeen, she married the Baron Ishimoto Keikichi, she seemed well on her way to fulfilling the subservient feminine role expected of an aristocratic woman. Her husband, however, insisted that Shidzue become a "new woman" of Japan; that she school herself for independence and activism in a world he hoped would come to reflect his ideals of socialism and Christian humanism. Trying to be the woman Keikichi demanded, in 1919 she left their two infant sons in the care of her mother and followed her husband to New York City to study the liberated ways of Western women. There she met the crusader for birth control Margaret Sanger, and determined that she, too, would become an advocate for family planning. This would be her specific contribution as she joined with other social and political activists who sought the liberation of Japanese women from feudal family law. But it was only one feature of her broader campaign for women's freedom and for social and political equality for everyone.

In the 1920s Shidzue saw her sisters subjugated by a family system that subordinated their lives to those of men, a government that barred them from political activities, and a social milieu that exploited their desire to work outside the home. The demand of the dominant society that women remain "good wives and wise mothers" belied the needs of urban Japan and ignored the long history of female factory workers. The industrial speed-up that followed World War I required a socially modern Japan employing both women and men. Like women in Europe and America, Shidzue decried the contradiction of a society requiring that women contribute their labor both at home and in business and industry, but kept them outside the political system, economically inferior and sexually exploited. Shidzue joined like-minded women and men in discussion of these topics, prepared pamphlets, wrote articles, and crusaded with others to bring about change. At this same moment she endured personal setbacks as her husband became more and more domineering and selfish.

By the mid-twenties, while Shidzue's thinking emphasized yet greater personal and public freedom, her husband, Keikichi, made a complete about-face. He demanded that Shidzue give up her liberated ways and become a traditional wife. Keikichi then joined imperialist adventurers seeking fortunes in China and Japan's Asian colonies, and by 1932 he had pledged his allegiance to the militarist goals of **Imperial Japan.** Abandoned, Shidzue was left to raise and provide for her teenage sons alone. She overcame this personal disappointment and sought her own freedom and independence. Even as her society turned more and more toward imperialism abroad and political suppression at home, she refused to surrender her vision of a democratic society where men and women were equal and human rights extended to everyone.

Amazingly, Shidzue broadened and refined her liberal views amid Japan's crises of the thirties as the country came more and more under the control of the militarist imperialists, a group she called "fascist." Her two additional opportunities for extended stays in America solidified her firm commitment to democracy, and her intimate association with the radical labor leader Katô Kanjû, which began in 1932, added a layer of European-inspired socialism to her eclectic belief system. Unlike Kanjû she was not a political theoretician, nor did she see any purpose to doctrinaire political practice, so she easily mixed her socialist thinking with the liberal democracy and romanticized free love adapted from her observations in America. Her primary interest was not the theory which imagined a just and equal society for both women and men, but, rather, the practice which would make it so. This activist approach led her to redoubling her efforts for birth control as a liberating practice for women. It also guaranteed that she would fight for women's political and economic rights which would assure their independence from family and/or male oppression. In all of this she struggled with her family, particularly her mother, husband, and other male relatives, who decried her actions as anathema to her aristocratic heritage and her proper place in the Japanese family and gender hierarchy.

Even when Japan's war with China and then the United States cut her off from her international contacts, she maintained a faith that eventually her country would come to its senses and the just world she envisioned would emerge. On a personal level, during this time of international crisis, Shidzue endured her own arrest, the government shutdown of her birth-control clinic, separation from her beloved Kanjû, and in the forties, the death of one son and the loss of the other to military service. In August 1945, she could proudly proclaim that she had survived the emotional and physical deprivation of war with her beliefs in women's liberation, democratic socialism, and political and social equality intact.

In the impoverished but stimulating immediate postwar period Katô Shidzue saw an opportunity to bring together the several strands of political and social thinking she had struggled with during the oppressive thirties. She was determined to play a major role in the democratic revolution that she believed peace and the American Occupation would force on Japan. Announcing her candidacy for the national legislature, the **Diet**, even before women were legally permitted such political rights, she began her postwar work for political and social democracy. Her crusade would include equal political rights for women and men, economic justice with particular attention to women and children, and international justice especially with regard to Japan's former colonies. The manifestation of these overall goals would take the form of practical action at the grassroots level, in national legislative campaigns, and through a commitment to international causes.

Shidzue would work within the Diet when this seemed the best course, but join with others in and out of political office and with Japanese officials and American Occupation authorities when this appeared advantageous. When necessary she would work alone. She would present her visions of democracy and social justice before groups at home and in international circles. In all of this she would not forget her promise in the 1920s to work for women's liberation through family planning and to this end she founded and remained the president of record of the Family Planning Federation of Japan until her death. Though not always successful in her quests, Shidzue's perspective was continuously before the public, who elected her to the Senate four times with large national margins. She died in December 2001 at the age of 104, after a lifetime of activism in which struggles against government oppression and social inequality brought substantive improvement to the lives of both Japanese women and men.

Acknowledgments

I greatly appreciate help in the completion of this book from Ashino Yuriko, Hosomi Mieko, Funabashi Kuniko,

Katoh Taki, and my editor, Peter Stearns; and financial support for research in Japan from the Japan Iron and Steel Endowment Fund and the Northeast Asia Council of the Association for Asian Studies. Acknowledgments are also given to the many reviewers who helped shape this work: Thomas Hegarty, University of Tampa; Sue Gonewald, Marist College; Edward Beasley, San Diego State University.

A Note on Names

In accordance with the usual practice, Japanese names appear in the order family name followed by given name. For stylistic reasons Katô Shidzue and other central characters are often referred to by given name alone.

HELEN M. HOPPER

Katô Shidzue

Learning from the East and the West

Shidzue's Parents: Hirota (Tsurumi) Toshiko, mother and Hirota Ritaro, father. Courtesy of Katô Shidzue.

On December 23, 1914, at age seventeen, Hirota Shidzue married Ishimoto Keikichi. It was a magnificent wedding appropriate to the joining of two wealthy, aristocratic families. The Baron Ishimoto's father, Lieutenant General Ishimoto Shinroku, had served the Meiji Emperor

1

with distinction in Japan's victorious war with Russia of 1904–1905. The emperor had rewarded his loyal subject by conferring on him the noble title of baron and, further, in 1911 had welcomed him as minister of war in Prime Minister (Prince) Saionji Kimmochi's cabinet. Unfortunately the baron died in 1912 after serving only briefly. He left a wife, six sons, of whom Keikichi was the eldest, and one daughter.

Shidzue was also from a distinguished, if untitled, family. Her father, Hirota Ritaro, was born in 1866 into a *samurai* family that served the Abe Clan in western Japan. After a childhood of private tutoring in classical Chinese and Japanese studies he entered the highly selective Imperial University in Tokyo to study science and mechanical engineering, thus accumulating the knowledge that would permit him to play a part in **Meiji** (1868–1912) Japan's remarkable industrialization. Shidzue described her father as "wearing a Western suit and hat, understanding English well, designing factories in modern style, but in his private life thoroughly imbued with the feudalistic ideology. He was during my childhood, and he still is (1935), a samurai, not with sword girded at his side, but with the engineer's ruler in his pocket." Hirota Ritaro was also honored by the government after the Russo-Japanese War. He was decorated by the emperor in recognition of his procurement of munitions for the military through his trading company in London. He was further celebrated by the Imperial University, which granted him an honorary doctorate of engineering and a university chair. It was he who sought out the Baron Ishimoto to be his daughter's husband, and it was he who convinced her of the appropriateness of the match.

Shidzue's mother, Tsurumi Toshiko, the eldest of ten children, came from a notable and highly educated family. She had attended a Canadian mission academy in her youth where she had studied English and other Western topics. In spite of this background, she exhibited no Western veneer whatsoever. In 1935 Shidzue described her as the quintessential traditional Japanese mother and wife. "My mother uses polite words only, never liking to pick up the vulgar words spoken in the street. She never betrays unpleasant feelings. 'Endurance' and 'repression' are her greatest ideals. She says to me, 'Endurance a woman should cultivate more than anything else. If you endure well in any circumstances, you will achieve happiness.'"

Growing up in comfort and style in Tokyo at the beginning of the twentieth century Shidzue was surrounded by quiet luxury, exposed to culture and learning, and provided with every convenience and opportunity appropriate to an educated girl in an upper-class environment. At the time of Shidzue's birth on March 2, 1897, the family still lived just outside the Imperial Palace, but soon after they moved to an exclusive area in Tokyo, very near the emperor, the government buildings, and the present-day Meiji Shrine. Shidzue described the area in her 1935 autobiography. "In the neighborhood of my father's home, all the residences occupy large tracts of land; from the gate to the house door there is usually a long avenue, and at the back of the house a spacious garden. Each house is surrounded by a six-foot wall of plaster or wood and only the top of the house can be seen from the street." In 1912 her father tore down his Japanese house and built a Western-style house designed by a German architect. He filled the house with Western furniture and inventions such as a piano, desks, a sewing machine, and other useful and aesthetic items brought home from his business trips to Europe. Shidzue enjoyed both Japanese and Western influences in her early education and material surroundings.

Shidzue's household included her parents, an elder brother, Kôichi, a younger brother, Yôji, twin younger sis-

Five of the six Hirota children, 1902. The three older children are dressed in Western clothing, which their father brought from Europe. Shidzue at five years old, her older brother Kôichi, younger brother Yôji, and twin sisters Kiyo and Kayo. Courtesy of Katô Shidzue.

ters, Kiyo and Kayo, and the youngest brother, Hirô. In addition, her mother's younger brother Tsurumi Yûsuke lived with the family for much of Shidzue's childhood. The large estate also accommodated a number of servants. During the summer all of the children and some servants went to Kamakura, the famous coastal seat of the powerful thirteenth-century **shogun**. It was a full day's journey from the Hirota's Tokyo house. The trip began by ricksha as several men pulled members of the family, trunks of belongings, clothing, books, and toys. "The ricksha men ran with speed on the flat roads along the moat under the hanging branches of willows or down hilly roads between the brick government buildings to Hibiya Park, but they were slow when they climbed hills, making zigzag curves while the persons who were riding would bend their bodies forward trying to cause these men less strain." The ride to the train station took forty minutes, and then the train ride to Kamakura with its eleven stops en route another three hours. Her grandfather's house was built on a cliff and from it one could see the entire town and the seashore. She remembered her summers as filled with swimming, nature walks, reading, and listening to her grandfather tell samurai stories of fighting for his lord just before the overthrow of the feudal **Tokugawa** Shogun in 1868.

In 1902, at the age of five, Shidzue was enrolled in the Peeresses' School, which had been founded by the empress just ten years after her husband, the Emperor Meiji, had established the Peers' School for boys in 1877. The Peeresses' School was an institution for children of the nobility and such others from upper-class families who were deemed suitable to associate with royalty. Until she was twelve Shidzue studied and played with members of the imperial family, learning the appropriate manners and etiquette for members of the overthrown feudal aristocracy, whose style of life endured within their own closed circle. In 1909 she graduated to the higher school, where for the next five years, until her marriage in 1914, she studied arithmetic, algebra, geometry, physics, chemistry, Japanese and foreign geography and history, and all forms of Japanese reading and writing as well as some Chinese. Most of her time, however, was spent on the arts appropriate for a proper wife; calligraphy, painting, drawing, music, sewing, embroidery, and cooking. In the few moments left she received training in ethics, with emphasis on loyalty to the emperor and the state, and in filial piety.

Shidzue has credited her early social training and mental awakening to two sources other than her formal education. It was her mother whom she considered the greatest influence on her aspiration to become a good wife and wise mother in accordance with the ideal of female subservience as expressed by the seventeenth-century neo-Confucian moralist Kaibara Ekken. On the other hand, she emphasized, "My young uncle, Tsurumi Yûsuke, was the one who first developed the intellectual side of my life." These two conflicting visions of training a young girl's mind and preparing her for adulthood represented the old and the new in twentieth-century Japan. It was her uncle's contribution that gave her the foundation for liberated thinking.

Tsurumi Yûsuke came to live in his older sister's home in 1908 when he was twenty-three and studying at the Imperial University. Shidzue was eleven when he first arrived and enjoyed his influence until she left home as Keikichi's wife. Uncle Yûsuke was Shidzue's great favorite. He passed along his beliefs in liberalism and a Christian-based humanism through his stories of human example drawn from ancient and modern histories of both the East and the West. Shidzue never tired of hearing these stories, which ranged from tales of ancient Japan, to the heroics of Joan of Arc, to the novel, *Uncle Tom's Cabin,* and to the political oratory of the American, William Jennings Bryan. Yûsuke talked about figures as diverse as Alexander the Great, Julius Caesar, Horatio, Lord Nelson, Florence Nightingale, and Abraham Lincoln. As a young primary-school child she was charmed and brought to tears by the stories. She was impressed by her uncle's belief that oratory such as Bryan's, heroism as illustrated by the Maid of Orleans, and democratic principles drawn from Lincoln would lead Japan to liberal democracy. He was no less inspiring for women's rights in the new Japan he envisioned for Shidzue and her siblings. She remembers him telling her "Be ambitious, grow to be an important woman of Japan!"

Uncle Yûsuke was a follower of Dr. Nitobe Inazô, the Christian humanist and interpreter of Japanese *bushidô,* or the way of the warrior. Married to an American from Philadelphia, Dr. Nitobe was at ease with Japanese and

Western customs and thought. He inspired both his circle of students, including Uncle Yûsuke and Keikichi, and a quiet observer, the teenaged Shidzue. As she recalls, "Motionless I watched him talking to these men about Goethe, Wordsworth and Tennyson. Of course I could not fully comprehend what they were saying or reading, but such names as Carlyle, Dante, Milton, Kant, Longfellow, and Victor Hugo became familiar to my ears, as I often sat listening to this great man." On these occasions Shidzue's mother let her help serve the male guests the evening meal. In deference to Western customs, her mother would bring out the white linens her father had brought back from London and Western as well as Japanese food served on fine Japanese pottery. Shidzue was being trained for her role as server of men by her mother, but the liberating mentoring of Uncle Yûsuke and the inspiration of Dr. Nitobe, her "reverend minister," were pulling her in a different direction.

Early Married Life

In 1914 when Shidzue's father brought her the good news that the Baron Ishimoto Keikichi's family sought her as his bride, she was far from delighted. Her father broke the news to her by saying, "I have something to tell you, Shidzue. Sit down please. You have finished your schooling now, so your mother and I are thinking about your future, wishing to make you happy by arranging a suitable marriage for you!" She responded by bursting into tears. Her tears came from "sweet regret at the dropping of curtains over my girlhood so soon." Her fears, however, were somewhat allayed by her Uncle Yûsuke's opinion of this man. "What a lucky child you are!" he told her. "You would be the most fortunate woman in Japan if you were to marry the young baron! . . . Baron Ishimoto is one of the brightest disciples of Dr. Nitobe." He then went on to explain that

Ishimoto was a student of **Christian humanism,** a gifted honor student at the Imperial University, who aspired to become a social reformer to help Japan's ill-treated laborers. To this end he was completing an engineering course and would use his education and talent for social causes.

Shidzue and Keikichi, ten years her senior, met in a formal ceremony and afterward each side gave the official go-between their consent to the match. As appropriate for an aristocrat, and according to the **Meiji Civil Code of 1898,** this was an arrangement between families, not individuals. Shidzue's parents were relieved that she freely agreed to the match, but her wishes were secondary at best. The marriage united two upper-class families. The Ishimotos could look forward to the extension of their line through a tie that could never be broken by the wife. As Shidzue explained, "A girl is taught to submerge herself in her husband's family, accepting her husband's ways with absolute willingness; but the husband and his family can divorce her for any simple reason."

The formal **Shintô** wedding, which followed an equally ritualistic betrothal ceremony, included the preparation of an extensive and expensive trousseau, befitting the baron's rank. This was comprised in part of bedding, cushions, clothing for all seasons and occasions, furniture, hair ornaments, and jewelry; it required four two-ton motor trucks to transfer the entire collection of goods to the baron's mansion five days before the wedding. At the conclusion of the ceremony on December 23, 1914, Shidzue would leave her family and join her husband to live in her mother-in-law's home and learn her ways. Her trousseau must provide all of her personal needs for much of her life to come. The wedding itself took place in the grand reception room of the Ishimoto mansion and in lieu of a Western-style marriage ritual, was solemnized by the "three-three-and-nine times" exchanging of the sake cup. For each event

over the course of the day Shidzue wore appropriate cere-
monial wedding kimono and hairstyle with all of the
expensive accompanying ornaments. It was a grand affair
out of the previous era. In deference to the modern period
the baron wore white tie, tails, and a top hat.

After graduation from the Imperial University and his
marriage to Shidzue, the baron joined the Mitsui Mining
Company as an engineer and was sent in January 1915 to
the island of Kyûshû to supervise workers in the Miike Coal
Mines. Married not yet a month, the bride and groom traveled by train along the coast parallel to the Inland Sea from
Tokyo to the southern tip of the island of Honshû, then
crossed the Straits of Shimonoseki by boat, and connected
with a train destined for northern Kyûshû where the mines
were located. Here they began their life among chimneys
puffing black smoke, the dust and dirt of the company
town, and the black underground coal mines. It was a star-
tling change from their accustomed rich cultural life amid
the best homes and gardens in Tokyo. Much to Shidzue's
surprise her executive husband did not move into a gentle-
man's office but conducted his work from the pit surrounded by common laborers and was, in fact, required to
do physical labor and not merely shuffle papers.

A further shock was their first home. She described the
company-owned residence as a "hut" with small four-mat
rooms and a narrow ladder to a tiny attic. The hut, which
was thatched with straw, had a minimal amount of elec-
tricity in the evening, but no private bath. The baroness had
to use the public bath like everyone else. One maid had
accompanied them to Kyûshû, and she proved invaluable,
working hard at scrubbing away the filth and, in general,
helping Shidzue to survive her wretched environment.
"Rats ran about freely regardless of the social rank of the
new occupants," Shidzue complained. "When it rained,
buckets, washtubs and bath towels of every kind were

quickly assembled to catch the water which dropped wherever it pleased through the leaky roof, upon our heads, into my closets where I kept the bed quilts and even on my beautifully polished chest of drawers brought from Tokyo."

Life in this mining area was miserable for the miners and their families and only somewhat better for Shidzue. Her husband began his breakfast of steamed rice, *misô* soup, and boiled eggs at five each morning. The hour was early but his meal more nourishing than those of his workers. While he ate, Shidzue read the Bible to him. He then walked to the mines and descended the pits to supervise his workers. Like them he had an hour for lunch at noon and then returned home at the end of the day so late that he only saw daylight when he worked the night shift. His salary was low and it was difficult to stretch it through the month, even though rent was free. In June 1917 Shidzue gave birth to their first son, Arata. About six months later Keikichi was recalled to Tokyo due to his deteriorating health.

The years 1915–1917 at the Miike Coal Mines were both miserable and enlightening for the privileged Shidzue. She was shocked by the tragic existence of the fifty thousand miners and their families and emotionally moved by those who managed to persevere amid continuous hardship. She had visited the cramped, stuffy, narrow pits and knew something about the adverse conditions her neighbors endured. She observed the women, burdened with many children but without the means to care for them. She saw the squalor in which they were forced to live and die. She heard even more from her husband about both the realities of the miners' dismal lives and the theories of why this was so, for his socialist ideals led him to fixed conclusions about the evils of capitalist management and its oppression of the people. Shidzue later claimed that her determination to take up the cause of birth-control education was based, in part, on these tragic impressions.

When the baron, baroness, and infant son returned to Tokyo they moved to Kamakura to be close to Keikichi's new job with a chemical laboratory, a subsidiary of the Mitsui Company. Their return coincided with the excitement caused by major international events. Among these, the most inspiring for Keikichi and other socialists in Tokyo was the Russian Revolution of October 1917. This was followed in the summer of 1918 by rice riots at home, which involved over a million people and were largely generated by disgruntled women suffering from high rice prices. The economic good times Japan enjoyed from shipping supplies and munitions to her allies during World War I were coming to an end. The winding-down of the war meant other changes as well, which frightened the conservative government. Farmers organized tenant unions, workers joined newly formed labor unions, and university students acted on left-wing theories. Fast moving events were causing liberals and radicals, especially student, labor, and intellectual leaders, to think forward to sweeping political and social changes within Japan.

Keikichi went obediently to his laboratory each day, but in his free time he studied labor problems and the relationship between the contribution of workers and the wealth created for owners like Mitsui in the new capitalist industries. Excitedly, he read the works of Marx, other socialist thinkers, and Russian literature. His study brought him to the conclusion that good intentions of even the best individuals were not adequate to rescue the poor for whom the world refused to show mercy. He must act.

Reeducation in the West

As Keikichi's thinking led him to more radical beliefs his dissatisfaction with the dull routine of his work increased. In an effort to understand the emotional and intellectual stress her husband was experiencing, Shidzue began to read some of the literature he suggested to her. She started to sympathize with his particular brand of humanism and could understand why he wanted desperately to do something more rewarding, more exciting, more pertinent to the changes he saw occurring in the world. She was not surprised when he finally acted.

Determined somehow to play a role in the earthshaking events, Keikichi decided to travel abroad and study at first hand the revolutionary socialist activities that were firing up the intellectuals he read and the workers they wrote for. Mundane family and company responsibilities paled in comparison with the possibility of joining the revolution. On February 13, 1919, Keikichi sailed for America, the first stop in his pursuit of radical transformation. He left behind a wife and two infants; for the preceding October his second son, Tamio, was born.

The excitement of the new environment completely enveloped Keikichi as he traveled about America. He sent home postcards and letters describing his experiences, and he invited his wife to join him in his revolutionary quest. He warned her, however, "Don't come abroad if you seek pleasure and new fashions in clothes or are planning to spend your time only at the theaters or motoring like other 'bourgeoises mesdames'. Come to me if you will educate yourself, to feed yourself with knowledge of the world, to prepare yourself to swim abreast the world's new tide." Shidzue, abandoned and lonely, made up her mind to leave her two babies and follow her husband to America. She sent the boys, Arata, then just past two, and Tamio, just one year old, with their maids to her family home in Kamakura, where they would be cared for by her mother. On August 15, 1919, she sailed for America. A month before she left she wrote in her diary of the pain of leaving her babies behind. She ended the entry, "I much prefer to stay with my darlings but I believe firmly that it is my duty to endure this trial of separation in order to study more while I am young so that some day in the future I can carry out a mother's duties to them in manifold measure." She had begun to reinterpret her role as traditional good wife and wise mother in the light of her husband's radical requirements for her life.

Shidzue's father accompanied her across the Pacific Ocean. Her husband met the ship in San Francisco and the three of them took a room at a hotel across the bay in Berkeley. While Shidzue listened, Keikichi then told her father of the things he had seen and the dreams he had dreamed for changing the lot of the laborer. She observed that "while both men had been educated at the same university and in the same field, one had strictly limited his interest to the sphere of mechanical power, and the other proposed to utilize its productive power in the interest of general human happiness. I recognized," she continued, "a thousand mile gap between the father and the son-in-law, and I thought that in that distance lay the progress of the younger generation."

The three then proceeded by train to New York City. Once there her father checked into a hotel in Washington Square and Keikichi took his wife to his cheap, dirty room where she encountered bed bugs, shabby furniture, and substandard facilities. The day after their arrival he showed her how, for a pittance, she could get a cup of coffee and a muffin at a Sixth Avenue cafe. She was scandalized. Why must she live in such an impoverished manner, she thought, given her station in life and her money in the bank? She was downcast and miserable. Her Uncle Yûsuke, also in New York, exclaimed that Keikichi had finally truly become a **Bolshevik** and, strangely, this comment made in jest, explained everything to Shidzue. One week later Keikichi took her to the Y.W.C.A. where he explained both to those in charge and to Shidzue that he wanted his wife to gain professional skills, learn English quickly, and thereby become an independent, self-supporting modern woman.

In October she registered for a secretarial course at the Ballard School in the Y.W.C.A. building. She worked so hard for the next few weeks on her stenography, book-keeping, secretarial duties, and typewriting that she was able to ignore the squalor of her living environment. Shidzue enjoyed the atmosphere of freedom and candor at the Ballard School, especially the fact that her teachers were all women. Though she had to use English, they made her feel comfortable asking any question, no matter how elementary. Shidzue was beginning to experience an intellectual freedom that would change her life.

Just one month later, October 1919, Keikichi went off to Washington, D.C., to the first meeting of the **International Labor Organization (ILO)**. Japan had been an ally with Britain, France, and the United States during World War I and consequently had had a seat, if a lowly one, at the Versailles Peace Conference during the previous winter and spring. In accordance with the Peace Treaty that Japan signed in June, the government agreed to permit the establishment of labor unions and was allowed, thereby, to join the ILO. For this first meeting, management manipulated the election of delegates and Japan's allotted voting slot was filled by an engineer instead of a worker. Baron Ishimoto, the socialist-humanist, resurrected his Mitsui engineering and management affiliation and his noble title and joined this representative and his other privileged compatriots.

Before he left New York City Keikichi encouraged his wife to find herself new quarters, thereby taking her first steps toward the independent life he envisioned for her. She advertised in the newspaper and the next day a southern American woman and her husband offered her a room in a more suitable middle-class area of New York. Thus the quality of her material life improved substantially, while her loneliness increased several fold after her husband left. Except for a brief interlude at Christmas, they were separated from October until Shidzue joined him in Europe early in the summer of 1920.

The year in America was a mixed one. Shidzue studied hard and learned both English and marketable secretarial skills, but she was intensely lonely for her family and for the friendship of other Japanese, and exhausted by the continuous need to speak in English. At one point in 1919, in direct defiance of her husband's command that she meet only with Americans, Shidzue had tea with the Japanese chief of the New York City branch of the Yokohama Specie Bank (present-day Bank of Tokyo). Their conversation, far from stiff and formal, turned quickly to the subject of love and, more specifically, the contrasting attitudes Japanese and American women held on this intimate topic. The banker told Shidzue that American women, unlike their Japanese counterparts, were interested in experiencing the freedom to enjoy all aspects of love. At that point he brought up Margaret Sanger, whom he described as a beautiful person who crusaded for birth control. Shidzue was completely in the dark. She had not heard of Margaret Sanger, nor did she know what birth control meant. Her companion went on to explain Sanger's crusade for planned children, as well as her attitudes toward free love. He also eagerly related stories about Sanger's battles with the authorities as she carried out her mission.

Shidzue had been quite taken with her frank discussion with the banker and decided to ask her husband's friend, Agnes Smedley, for further information about the curious and remarkable woman, Margaret Sanger. Smedley, who had been held in prison for possible seditious acts until the end of World War I, was one of Shidzue's few acquaintances in New York City. Happily for Shidzue, in January 1920, Smedley was in charge of Sanger's new journal, *Birth Control Review,* and the two American activists were close friends. Smedley spoke with Sanger about the Japanese woman whom she described as exotic and independent and married to a radical. Sanger, intrigued, invited the Baroness Ishimoto to be her guest of honor at a tea held at her apartment on an icy winter day.

When Sanger greeted the baroness at her door on January 17, she shattered the mental image Shidzue had formed during the earlier conversation with the banker. Sanger was not strong-minded, big-boned, manlike, with short hair and a large voice, as she had imagined. After all, wouldn't these be the mental and physical characteristics of someone who fought the authorities, the Japanese woman thought. Instead Margaret Sanger was beautiful, had thick, abundant hair, big blue eyes, a lovely voice and a warm manner.

The inspiration emanating from this one meeting was dramatic. Sanger's personal demeanor, her birth-control message to mothers, and her loudly proclaimed attitudes about the fulfillment of women's emotional and sexual desires all made an impact on the dejected young Japanese woman. Whether Shidzue did, in fact, determine at that moment that birth-control education would become her particular social cause, she certainly felt the desire somehow to free Japanese women from male oppression and to improve the quality of married women's lives.

The new information conveyed by Sanger and her friends meshed readily with Shidzue's husband's humanistic teachings and his insistence on her own acquisition of independence and self-sufficiency. She saw a connection between male sexual domination and female social and economic dependence. Here was the place for her to start.

A woman would never be free, she reasoned, as long as she did not achieve independence. She described her new goals in a school letter-writing exercise. "I believe that every woman whether she belongs to the upper class or to the lower class, married or single, should not be dependent upon a man, economically or intellectually." During the next two years she would tie the achievement of female independence to a woman's need to control the size of her family. In her husband's absence Shidzue had learned the lessons he had forced on her very well.

By contrast, the baron's frenzied travels to Mexico, back to America, and off to Europe, all in search of an understanding and application of Christian humanism, proved disillusioning. His ultimate goal had been to travel to the new Soviet Union, to observe the manifestation of his revolutionary beliefs in all their glory. On January 3, 1920, he sailed for Europe. Once there, his primary goal was to enter the USSR and meet with Lenin and Trotsky, who were "carrying out the socialism which has shaken the world since Karl Marx advanced his new ideas." His dream, however, became a nightmare. In spite of introductions from Japan's best-known socialist, Katayama Sen, and American radicals, such as the labor leader Bill Haywood of the International Workers of the World, Soviet officials refused to issue him a visa. The primary obstacle was his title; a revolutionary could hardly be addressed as baron.

By the time Shidzue joined her husband in England early that summer, he was sullen and irretrievably distraught. He gave no sign of passion or even interest in their reunion. His disillusionment was plain, and this had changed his character irrevocably. Shidzue was determined to enjoy her new experience despite her husband's dark manner, and, in truth, became enchanted with her post–World War I tour of Europe. Every place—Paris, London, Rome—was new and exciting. There were moments of returned joy to their marriage, but there was no doubt that Keikichi had begun to lose his romantic idealism just at the time that Shidzue had discovered the personal ideal of free love and the public social cause of women's liberation.

At the end of the summer husband and wife returned home. The Ishimotos' circle of friends were interested in the couple's exotic travels. Shidzue and Keikichi became newsworthy and were introduced about as representatives of the "new man" and "**new woman**" of Japan. Keikichi wrote articles for the newspaper about his exotic experiences and for a brief moment forgot his disappointments.

Shidzue had not forgotten her promises to herself to seek economic independence and to propagate birth-control education, but she had to find some way to accomplish this within the constraints of her aristocratic social class and family responsibilities. Reality and dreams did not mesh easily. She found a part-time job as private secretary at the Y.W.C.A., which would allow her to care for her sons, earn a small income, and use her new professional skills, but would not cause opposition at home. In less than a year her supervisor returned to America and Shidzue returned full time to her traditional role of wife and mother. She appeared to have taken a step backward.

Keikichi, meanwhile, found his dreams stifled by his tiresome work environment. In apparent conflict of interest, but in accordance with his sympathies for the worker, he joined the mining division of the new All Japan Labor Union, where he established a subgroup to study labor questions. Soon, however, he recognized that his labor interests and his role as a Mitsui engineer/manager were antithetical to his own beliefs about the disaccord that existed between the interests of the mine owners and laborers. Mitsui's management, as well, found Keikichi's two roles at odds. He was informed that his union work was inappropriate and was reproved by his superiors. He resigned his job. Although, for the moment, he had adequate wealth whether he worked or not, he needed a focus, albeit not employment that conflicted with his ideology. He found his answer in the establishment of a book store that stocked imported foreign books. Keikichi, still discontented, was establishing a pattern of both financial failure and instability in his professional life. This was just one of the first signs of an inconstancy that would push him from project to project, casting him as a wanderer with uncertain focus.

Shidzue's determination to gain economic independence would not permit her to retreat into the traditional female role for long, and so she too became a shopkeeper. Fortuitously, a friend who imported yarn from America convinced her that she could profitably run a retail yarn shop. With great vision she opened the Minerva Yarn Store which sold yarn, finished products knitted on a piecework basis by women working in their homes, and provided space for a knitting school in an adjacent room. Her shop also provided employment for a few of her upper-class friends. An aristocrat playing the role of a merchant was news and the Tokyo newspapers ran feature stories about the wife of the Baron Ishimoto and her new store. She was pleased with the free advertising, but the baron's brothers criticized Shidzue, saying that her independent behavior was inappropriate for an upper-class woman. They told her that she should be home performing the role of **good wife** and **wise mother** rather than imitating the lowly merchant class and becoming the common subject of news articles. Shidzue was experiencing the conflict between the freedom she had learned in America and the behavioral expectations for her aristocratic status. She was also experiencing turmoil at home as her business prospered and her husband's failed.

By 1922, Shidzue, who had been trained in the traditional ways of a lost era, had become radically reeducated toward thoughts of liberation for herself and for her female compatriots. She had begun to weave an activist future from the intellectual and emotional threads she had taken up in the West in 1920 and 1921. The fabric would take the entire decade to weave, and its design and character would change in accordance with personal associations and national policies, but the pattern was clear. On the personal level, economic independence would become both a cause and a necessity; intimate relations with a man would have to include mutual respect, romance, and equally satisfying sexual love; and child raising, though it would continue to be an important focus, would not be all consuming. On the public level, social action for birth control would be intertwined with a determination to free women from oppression and ensure their equality with men; international cooperation would take precedence over national self-interest; and political and social action within a democratic framework would be demanded to achieve the first two goals. Within these contexts Shidzue would find that she would build on her association with Margaret Sanger and with other Americans, and she would make strategic use of her growing knowledge of Western culture and the English language. Facing both East and West she would be challenged by personal and public excitement as well as turmoil and confusion in the decades to come. Her way would not be smooth nor without personal tragedy, but her influence and contribution both nationally and internationally would be substantial.

Pioneering for Women's Rights in the Twenties

Baroness Ishimoto Shidzue, her husband, Baron Ishimoto Keikichi and their sons, Arata and Tamio at home. Courtesy of Katô Shidzue.

The 1920s in Japan is often called the era of **Taishô** democracy. This label combines the name of the Taishô Emperor (1912–1926), son of the Meiji Emperor with a belief that the nation was beginning to embrace democra-

Shidzue addresses the Ashiô miners at the invitation of labor leader Katô Kanjû, 1923. Posters in background have slogans such as "Prepare for May Day," "Birth Control for Working Women." Courtesy of Katô Shidzue.

tic ideals. This can be somewhat confusing since the ill Taishô Emperor was replaced by his son, Hirohito, as regent in 1922, and since the twenties also includes the early years of the **Shôwa** Emperor's (Hirohito) reign. Some historians have characterized this decade as democratic by hightlighting liberal and democratic tendencies that appeared or were intensified after World War I. This analysis emphasizes the growth of political parties, and the democratic activism of labor unions, university students, women's groups, and literary circles. Also, midway through the decade the Diet passed a law providing for universal manhood suffrage that anticipated a future of increased citizen participation in government. Internationally, during this period, Japan joined the major powers in conferences directed toward arms reduction and, in general, participated in the new approach to foreign policy called the "Washington system," which was meant to replace the prewar dependence on secret national alliances. Japan held a permanent seat in the Council of the **League of Nations,** and Nitobe Inazô, Shidzue and Keikichi's mentor, became its under secretary-general. During the twenties, Japan's economy also became more global as the government attempted to create a favorable climate for business.

Culturally the Japanese were learning from Europe and America as well as adding their own vision to twenties thinking and writing. A universal education requirement for children and an expanding higher school system provided educated men and women for the urban labor force. An impressive university system including both public and private institutions, even some advanced schools for women, provided a large pool of educated men for civil service, the law, industrial management, and engineering and of men and women for careers in writing, teaching, social work, and medicine. Japan seemed to be positioning itself for a greater role among the world's capitalist nations.

When Shidzue returned from America she, like many of her Tokyo compatriots, was excited by the democratic activism in evidence. She could see a future working for women's rights. While abroad she had determined that family planning would be her primary cause, and the times seemed right for her to pursue this. She believed promotion of birth control was a necessary step toward freeing women from Japan's patriarchal legal code, which subordinated all women to their male relatives, father first, and then husband. The time seemed good for launching a birth-control movement, for the public was already interested in the subject and eager to learn more. On a more personal level she saw this as a project that could bring her closer to her discontented husband.

Keikichi, always looking for something to fasten his footloose existence to, began to study the issue of birth control, and to discuss it with associates who came to the house. This group of men, which included the labor leader Katô Kanjû, discussed the connection between the impoverished living conditions of workers, their fight for just wages and benefits, and their inability to control the size of their families. Birth-control education based on a scientific study of family limitation, and its relationship to more prosperous and healthy workers, seemed necessary to any discussion of labor reform.

Meanwhile, Shidzue both served as hostess, in the manner taught her by her mother, and acted independently. She had already gained fame through an *Asahi Newspaper* article of September 1920, which linked her with Margaret Sanger. It seems that during her stay in New York she had told an *Asahi* reporter about her meeting with Sanger, and believing this newsworthy, he had sent off a report which was published just before Shidzue returned home. In the spring of 1921 Shidzue published her own two-part article in a Tokyo newspaper on the importance of birth-control education. Birth control was a hot issue.

During the summer of 1921, Shidzue sent an essay to Margaret Sanger, which she published in the September issue of *The Birth Control Review.* The article emphasized the importance of bringing population growth into sync with the limited resources available in Japan by limiting births and thus improving living standards for individual families. Ishimoto's most poignant plea, however, was "for the emancipation of women. . . . The Japanese woman must be liberated to develop freely. . . . Japanese women must have time and money to seek self development," she proclaimed. She further stated that women spent an inordinate amount of time devoted to child rearing and serving their husbands and in-laws. Women were forced to sacrifice all discretionary money to the needs of their children, leaving nothing for their own cultural and educational advancement. Birth control, then, was essential to the physical and spiritual freedom of women.

On May 10, 1922, Shidzue and her husband gathered together a group of interested people for a mid-day discussion about propagation of birth-control ideas in Japan. Their neighbor, the missionary Elizabeth Coleman, was included to provide firsthand information from America. Excited by this event, Coleman immediately wrote to her friend Margaret Sanger praising the charming Baroness Ishimoto, who was called "control" by students at the university, adding that one feels very glad to have a leader like her. She concluded, "The Ishimotos are so unusually radical and progressive for Japan."

The Ishimotos were not the first to discuss birth control in Japan nor were Shidzue's articles the first to attract the public's attention. In fact, interest in this subject had boomed after the end of World War I, generated by the same economic problems that brought about the 1918 rice riots, and by the realization that Japan's population was increasing well beyond the capacity of its natural resources. Women's magazines, newspapers, and other publications featured numerous articles on birth control, beginning as early as 1918. Articles in the well-circulated *Housewife's Friend* ran the gamut from advice about and ads for contraceptives, to discussions of ways to prevent venereal disease. Articles appeared about the work of Marie Stopes in England, well known because of her residence in Japan early in the century. Once in a while the lesser-known American, Margaret Sanger, was also mentioned. By the time Shidzue's articles appeared, birth control was a subject that had generated great interest, if little understanding, among the literate and intellectual classes. Consequently, the guests at the Ishimoto house in May were not being introduced to this topic for the first time. The practical outcome of this meeting was the establishment of the **Birth Control**

League of Japan, which was patterned after the plans for the soon to be established American Birth Control League.

Sanger Aids the Cause

Shidzue, meanwhile, prepared for a visit from her mentor, Margaret Sanger, who had accepted an invitation from the magazine *Reconstruction* to visit Japan in 1922 and lecture on birth control. In 1920 the magazine had established a five-year program to bring an outstanding world figure once each year to give public lectures. They had already presented Albert Einstein and Bertrand Russell. Shidzue was overjoyed; it was a dream come true. The word went out in headlines everywhere, "Margaret Sanger, Birth Control Pioneer, Is Coming."

Sanger's shipmates on the voyage included Japanese military and foreign office officials such as Foreign Minister Shidehara Kijûrô, who would become prime minister after World War II, and Admiral Katô Tomosaburô, navy minister. These government luminaries were returning from their tough and disappointing bargaining over naval reductions at the nine-power international treaty conference in Washington, D.C.

When the ship docked on March 10th, Sanger's reception was less than hospitable. Urged on by a large block of conservatives in the **House of Peers,** the upper house of the Japanese Diet, authorities refused to permit her a visa to land. Many in the civilian government as well as military leaders saw Sanger's visit, which directly followed the forced treaty reduction of the Japanese naval fleet by the more powerful British and Americans at the Washington Conference, as yet another attempt by the West to limit Japan's power and prestige. The only difference was that this time it would be limitation of people rather than ships. Consequently, the military sympathizers among those in power opposed lectures on techniques that could be used to limit births. Such information might subvert Japan's national policy of strengthening its industrial and military might.

Sanger was met, as well, by friends. "Baron Ishimoto fortunately was there early to advise me. . . ," she wrote in her Diary.

> Baroness Ishimoto came in her native costume. Very tall and lovely to look at. Speaking clear and fine English. Also present was a delegation of six women representing the Women's Movement in Japan. These adorably perfect doll women came in costume, bowing so stately and courteously from the waist to the floor almost, took ones thoughts away from the difficulties of officials & the trials of the day and brought first the perfumes of a fairy land with gnomes & delightful wise old ladies to the realization that these little new women in Japan are the instruments to carry out the real dreams of an emancipated womanhood in Japan.

And thus Sanger began her affectionate, if sometimes condescending, relationship with the Japanese people, both real and mythical, who accorded her more adoration and respect than she ever received at home.

Only after Sanger had signed an agreement not to speak publicly about birth control was she finally permitted to leave the ship. According to this document she could not explain practical methods of contraception, suggest how to obtain birth-control literature, or introduce birth control as a method of limiting population in any public forum. The authorities privately admitted that there was not much they could do about prohibiting these banned topics in small gatherings at private homes. She participated in a whirlwind of social events at which she privately discussed prohibited topics while publicly lecturing on acceptable topics. Reporters followed her everywhere quoting her daily in their newspapers. During most of her activities the Baroness Ishimoto, at whose Tokyo home Sanger stayed, was at her side, sometimes as translator, but primarily as hostess and friend. At all public events, which included dinner parties, teas, and receptions, a large contingent of police, present to monitor her words, also joined the elite company of guests who gathered to listen to this celebrity.

During her stay in Japan, Sanger appeared impressed by the titled male elite interested in her cause. She seemed less certain of the accomplishments and future potential of Japan's new woman, and was highly stereotypical in her descriptions of even the women with professional qualifications.

Sanger's first dinner party was held in Yokohama with eight Japanese men. The next day she had one of those private talks without police listening in. "Dr. Kaji told of the methods of B.C. he found successful—plain soft Japanese paper folded & inserted against cervix—then as this absorbs the sperm it is removed & a clean piece wet in antiseptic solution & wiped the vagina dry & clean. 1000 cases no failures." Later that day Sanger met at the Peers Club with "a select group. We spoke very frankly—talked of methods & the art of love It was very inspiring to hear their questions & to hear their perfect English. Baroness Ishimoto sat throughout the discussion very bravely." She enjoyed a dinner with twenty-five of the men, "no wives."

This stimulating and frank camaraderie with upper-class men whom she saw as her intellectual equals could be contrasted with her descriptions of Japanese women whose "doll-like" demeanor, attractive attire and "tiny" stature impressed her. Even when she lectured to fifty nurses and female doctors she disparagingly wrote that they were "a very insignificant looking group of nurses and only the lead physician looked really intelligent—this (female) doctor thought that using the **pessary** caused irritation—very reactionary, behind some of the men physicians."

Just before she left Japan Sanger concluded, "The women here are too low voiced to ever do anything. They are trying too hard 'to be or not to be' proper. One hears much of the 'New Woman' but one seldom sees her." This evaluation of Japanese women, like those Sanger would make in the thirties, shows that she was not as observant of the people Shidzue had gathered to talk with her, or knowledgeable of the variety of new women actively discussing women's roles, as she believed. Most certainly, she had underestimated Ishimoto Shidzue and her feminist allies.

Sanger's visit was a triumph. She was constant copy for reporters and revered by all who hosted her, and she even received adulation from some officials who prevented her from speaking publicly about birth control. For the baroness the American was a godsend, a morale builder, an inspiration with practical advice and materials for advancing her chosen cause. Ishimoto Shidzue, "Madame Control," was now given a new title by the newspapers which was echoed loudly by the members of the public; she was called "The Margaret Sanger of Japan."

Another Mentor from America

Tokyo of 1922 was an exciting and exhilarating place, and it had a forward-looking mayor who wanted to make it livable and modern as well. The mayor, Viscount Gotô Shimpei, was one of Japan's most revered Meiji/Taishô statesmen. After completing a medical degree he went to the University of Berlin where he studied Germany's public health system. He returned to Tokyo in 1892 a firm believer in **Bismarck's state socialism.** From this point on he continuously held important bureaucratic positions, at both the local and national level, from which he worked paternalistically to improve living conditions for the people.

In 1910 Count Gotô's daughter, Yoshi, married the new Imperial university graduate Tsurumi Yûsuke, who was to gain national recognition as a bureaucrat, politician, intellectual, writer, novelist, lecturer, and unofficial ambassador to the United States. This, of course, was Uncle Yûsuke who had so significantly influenced Shidzue. In 1918, when Gotô was in America consulting at the New York Bureau of Municipal Research, he became acquainted with the famous historian Charles A. Beard, one of the bureau's researchers, and with his wife and co-author, Mary Beard. The following year when Tsurumi was in New York, he also met the Beards. Thus, when the city of Tokyo unexpectedly came into a large sum of money to establish a Bureau of Municipal Research, both Gotô and his son-in-law, Tsurumi, thought of Charles Beard. In February 1922, Mayor Gotô officially invited Beard to come to Japan to offer advice on modernization of the city's government and services. Tsurumi, who was once again in New York, acted as go-between. Convincing Beard to come was not difficult, for both he and his wife were eager to visit the Far East. More important, Charles was excited and challenged by the mammoth project that urban planning for a modern Tokyo would present.

Charles, Mary, and their two children arrived in Tokyo on September 14th. During their six-month stay, Charles generously lectured throughout the country, consulted with Gotô and other Tokyo officials, discussed municipal planning with several mayors, and, in spare moments, enjoyed thoroughly the entertainment and cultural displays provided him and his family by the grateful elite of Japan's officialdom. When he lectured outside Tokyo, he was accompanied by Tsurumi as his translator and confidant. Meanwhile,

Mary Beard was entertained by Ishimoto Shidzue, acting at her uncle's behest. Shidzue's knowledge of English and her familiarity with the West made her a perfect host. As a bonus, Shidzue was a representative Japanese new woman and was, therefore, of intellectual interest to Mary Beard, an observer and writer about women's lives.

The meeting between Mary Beard and Shidzue had been fortuitous. In the future there would be yet another contact in America and a new mentor from whom to learn Western ways. In the thirties Mary would be an important conduit for writing projects, which would help to keep Shidzue intellectually stimulated and economically solvent during the traumatic years of militaristic repression.

A New Political Freedom for Women

Shidzue and other activist new women were exhilarated in 1922 finally to be able to organize politically without fear of government interference or possible arrest. They spent the next few years organizing and joining groups as they tested the political freedoms the Diet had finally voted them. Before this time the 1890 revision of Article Five of the Police Security Regulations, and its amendment of 1900, had prohibited women from joining political parties, organizing or participating in political groups, assembling or joining meetings that discussed political topics, or acting in any manner that might be considered political. In fact, women had been illegal political participants for years, especially since World War I when the numbers of activist women's groups had increased dramatically. But these groups had existed at the pleasure of the authorities. The Home Ministry, which controlled the police and other bureaucratic divisions, had the power to interpret and execute the many public peace and police laws and ordinances, to the detriment of individual women and groups that the authorities deemed political. In February 1922, the Diet amended the Public Peace Police Law to permit women to attend and organize political meetings and discussions. This milestone recognized the contribution of women activists and inspired them to take further steps toward the social and political reform necessary to secure full civil rights.

In May 1922, Shidzue and a few close friends formed a private society to discuss social, political, and literary questions of the day. This group, called the Coming Light Society, was made up of both men and women, many of whom were artists. It included, among other writers, the popular and successful novelist and social critic Arishima Takeo. His novels *A Certain Woman* and *Grab Love with Abandon* had established him as an intellectual concerned about the new woman's social and sexual life. He was particularly lauded for his ability to delineate the conflicts and confusions which the new woman experienced as she sought sexual and personal freedom. In his writings he philosophized about the contradiction that necessarily arose between morality and instinctive living, and both revered and criticized what he termed, in English, the impulsive life. A second important member of the Coming Light Society was Shidzue's dear friend, Hatano Akiko, an editor at the popular women's magazine *Women's Review.* Hatano and Arishima caused a scandal in March 1923 that implicated Shidzue and scarred her birth-control movement.

Arishima, a widower, and Hatano, married to a prominent businessman, had, for some time, been involved in a secret love affair. Shidzue, as Hatano's confidante, had discussed the illicit liaison in the context of Japan's male-biased adultery laws, which automatically punished the woman, and the code of Japan's new woman, which celebrated sexual and emotional freedom. Both Hatano and Shidzue had been heavily influenced by Arishima's writings about love, and by the more sexually explicit foreign writings of Margaret Sanger, her British lover Havelock Ellis, and Marie Stopes. Shidzue said later that she had advised her friend to end the affair. Neither Hatano nor Arishima, however, had the power to break off their relationship and their sad solution was a double love suicide.

Hatano left a note for Shidzue, who was then implicated and met with public disapproval for not having restrained her friend. In the end Shidzue suffered ostracism by many in her upper-class social circle, and notoriety in the newspapers. Furthermore, her advocacy of birth control was criticized by those who associated the practice of birth control with "comfortable" sex, declaring that bourgeois women prevented conception so that they could "play." The entire affair was a sobering one for Shidzue, who not only lost a dear friend, but found herself the focus of unwanted celebrity and her cause in disrepute. Once again her aristocratic status betrayed her egalitarian political leanings. Moreover, she was angry that society permitted illicit sexual alliances on the part of men but held adultery by women to be a heinous moral transgression as well as a legally prosecutable crime. She would have cause to ponder both issues, social class divisions and adultery laws, more personally in the future.

Another member of Shidzue's Coming Light Society was Katô Kanjû, labor leader, who lectured to the group on "The History of the Japanese Labor Movement" and "Problems of Women Factory Workers." He had been a regular visitor to the Ishimoto household during Keikichi's attempts at labor organizing. Kanjû, also a member of the Birth Control Study Group, was respected and his company enjoyed by both Ishimotos. After one of the Coming Light Society discussions in 1923, Kanjû invited Shidzue to join his labor organizers and speak to the miners and their wives about birth control at the Ashiô Copper Mines, located to the north, near Nikkô, about eight hours by train from Tokyo. Shidzue agreed, though she had never lectured to a group of workers before and was apprehensive. Happily her friend, neighbor, and associate in the birth-control movement Elizabeth Coleman volunteered to accompany her. This quieted Shidzue's fears.

The two meetings held at the mines on March 31 and April 1, 1923, drew large crowds, for the miners were curious as to whether the baron's wife could understand the pain of such lowly people. Drawing from her experiences in the Miike Coal Mines in Kyûshû seven years earlier, she spoke about unplanned children, the suffering of women, and the impoverishment of families. Four days later she wrote to Sanger to tell her about the event. "Two large meetings . . . at the theater of Ashiô town . . . were attended by 1200 to 1300 miners and their wives. I gave the address on the subject of Birth Control, and even though I was interrupted several times by the police, I succeeded in delivering the thought which I wanted to propagate. . . . I was called the 'Japanese Sanger.'"

Shidzue later called this event a turning point in her life. She had conquered her fear of speaking before workers and their wives and had braved the possible wrath of the authorities, who were ever present and seeking an opportunity to halt the propagation of radical ideas. And she proved to the impoverished miners that an aristocratic woman could sympathize with them and suggest practical solutions to their plight. In the twenties democracy was given lip service and the presentation of liberal ideas, even those of the birth-control and labor movements, was acceptable, though carefully monitored.

Upheaval by Nature and Man

On September 1, 1923, Tokyo suffered a cataclysmic earthquake, one of the most devastating natural disasters in history. It was followed by hundreds of aftershocks and wildfires, which rampaged out of control consuming all wooden structures in the way. Fortunately, the entire Hirota-Tsurumi-Ishimoto clans escaped any serious injury or loss in this disaster, which killed over one hundred thousand people and destroyed much of Tokyo.

After the earthquake Keikichi could not seem to find solace in his failing book business, nor could he think of any other endeavor that would be fulfilling. His answer, as usual, was to travel, in effect to run away. In the spring of 1924, Shidzue closed her successful business and once again the couple left their two sons, Arata, almost seven, and Tamio, five and a half, and sailed for America and then Europe. In the fall, after nine months of excitement abroad, they finally returned home to face each other and life without the glamour and constant stimulation of travel and the excitement of international companions. There was little doubt that Shidzue's marriage was failing her expectations of Western-style equality and romantic love.

By contrast, the year 1925 was an exciting one for many of Shidzue's urban compatriots. It was filled with economic promise and romantic adventure for women who dreamed of personal independence and sexual freedom. Many middle-class women were finding jobs, sometimes to provide needed income for a family but sometimes simply to give themselves a sense of independence and freedom. Both women and men were reading literature and articles that praised the new liberties urban women were experiencing, and even conservative women who remained in traditional roles enjoyed vicariously the autobiographical and fictional experiences that the new writers portrayed. The first chapter of Miyamoto Yuriko's novel *Nobuko* was published in a popular magazine in 1924. It centered on Miyamoto's unfulfilling marriage and her search for personal independence and freedom from family duty and responsibility. That same year Tanizaki Junichirô's novel *A*

Fool's Love was serialized in the *Osaka Asahi Newspaper.* His primary character was a female, Naomi, who seduced readers with her sexual freedom and total lack of personal and familial responsibility. These works and many others became popular as both women and men of this period were intrigued by the sexual attributes of the variously described new woman and modern girl.

Politically, women were encouraged by the passage of the universal manhood suffrage law in March 1925. This gave them hope for their own cause as they optimistically saw women's enfranchisement as the obvious next step in Japan's democratic development. Countervailing laws, also passed in March, did not seem to attract much interest among the women, but would loom large in Ishimoto Shidzue's life a few years into the future. These were the **Peace Preservation Law,** which added further weight to previous regulations, and laws designed to permit the state to control the political and social activities of its citizens and, thus, protect the nation from the negative consequences of "**dangerous thoughts.**" This was a terrifying term left undefined in the legal statutes. It could and would be expanded over the next fifteen years to include any expression or activity the government believed threatening to its authority. At best, democracy had a tenuous foothold in Japan.

Ishimoto Shidzue found it difficult to share in the excitement of the mid-twenties. She limited her political activities to brief gatherings with women's rights groups and retreated further into her home. In the beginning her withdrawal was balanced by her desire to urge her depressed husband into an active political life. When his subsequent attempt to gain the support of his fellow aristocrats for election to the House of Peers failed, the distressed Keikichi abandoned his family responsibilities. He sought solace in adventure and, on occasion, employment in distant parts of the Japanese Empire, first Korea, later Northern China, and Manchuria.

Keikichi's activities seemed to foreshadow his nation's imperial incursions to come.

Shidzue remained at home with her growing sons, occasionally joined by Keikichi, who would return briefly in a whirl of apparent glory. For Shidzue, the late twenties was a period of decreasing wealth and increasing depression. She described this period as one of emotional and economic breakdown. She had permitted her husband Keikichi to determine the course of their lives since the mid-twenties in the hopes of saving her marriage. Somehow Keikichi, who ten years before had insisted that Shidzue become a free and independent woman, had made an about-face and required that she play the traditional role of subservient wife to her **feudal** lord. As Keikichi continued to roam abroad, it became more and more evident that he had abandoned his family responsibilities, and Shidzue could no longer love or respect him. She decided it was time to rejoice in her independence, determine her own future, and return to an active life.

Renewed Activism

To Shidzue and other family-planning activists, Japan of 1929 appeared to be hospitable to birth control as one approach to solving the recent population upsurge and the poverty accompanying that increase. Clinics sprang up all over Tokyo in response to a declaration by the assistant mayor that birth control was the best hope for decreasing the high infant mortality and increasing the health prospects for those in the lower classes. As Shidzue reported to Sanger, "The Health Department of the city of Tokyo is considering setting up birth control clinics in the Municipal Health Advice Stations, and eight have already been established in the slum districts in Tokyo." She continued that there were already thirty-two social workers who were teaching the poor the evil of prolific births, advising them to use contraception, and sending them to the clinics for appropriate instruction. Shidzue emphasized that B.C. was now a politically acceptable topic, for it was the majority party, the conservative **Friends of the Government Party,** which proclaimed that birth control was an appropriate means to solve Japan's population problems. The party's decision to advocate birth control, in spite of opposition by its leader, was based on population and food pressures, and on the growing problem of venereal disease in the military. A cabinet report recommended creation of offices that would provide for consultation on marriage, birth, and contraception; regulation of improper advertisement, sale, and distribution of contraceptives; and research into eugenic aspects of contraception.

In 1930 it appeared that the birth-control movement would receive both endorsement and substantive help from government bureaus. Government enthusiasm for birth control, however, proved fickle. By January 10, 1931, the Home Ministry issued a qualifying directive stating that intrauterine contraceptives could not be sold, displayed, or stored for sale because they were likely to cause injury. The document further stated that birth control was a private matter and that the government did not intend either to condemn or condone the use of contraceptives. (This was quite a liberal position compared to the United States' Comstock laws, which prohibited both contraceptives and birth-control literature.) Birth control was not outlawed in Japan, contraceptives such as condoms could be sold, and intrauterine devices could be provided in clinics; however, the government appeared to be modifying its previous wholehearted support. This public hesitancy motivated Shidzue and her associates to reform and expand their private endeavors in birth-control education. Accordingly on January 17, 1931, the Birth

Control League of Japan held an organizational meeting and Shidzue was named the first president.

The schizophrenic response of local government to birth-control propagation mirrored the bureaucratic and legislative confusion in larger circles over just what direction Japan would move in the new decade. There was no uniformity of purpose and, consequently, much contention at all levels of authority and among the various factions within society. Economic panic, followed by recession, and then depression caused severe hardship in both the cities and countryside. Political parties, which had held such democratic promise, seemed unable to respond creatively and became suspect. The prime minister was first of one persuasion and then another as power and policy shifted from more liberal economic strategies to harsher ones, from increased international hostility, especially toward China, to greater cooperation and then back again. At the beginning of the thirties it was simply uncertain just what the future of Japan might be.

I I I

Pursuing Freedom Amid Hostilities

Shidzue's return to public activism did not erase her problems at home. By 1931 she knew that her marriage was over. The couple's problems went beyond lack of love. Keikichi's activities had become erratic as he moved from Tokyo to Korea to Manchuria to China seeking employment and emotional fulfillment. Politically his thinking had moved from far left to far right. Clearly, Keikichi had joined the ranks of those calling for colonial expansion. He was eager to be a part of the glorious future he saw for the Japanese Empire. Shidzue, on the other hand, remembered her taste of freedom and her desire to liberate other women from family oppression. After five years of catering to her husband's authority, she determined to seek a free and independent life.

Abandoned for Imperialist Glory

In the fall of 1931 Shidzue was dismayed and depressed by both her husband's adventures and her nation's act of conquest. On September 18, 1931, Japan's **Kwantung Army** had contrived hostilities in **Manchuria** by blowing up a section of the South Manchurian Railroad. Three days

41

later the Japanese army widened the war by occupying the provincial government in Kirin and then Mukden. Taken by surprise, the government in Tokyo blustered about looking for a solution to the "Manchurian Question" that would not cause a war with the USSR or any other Western power. Eventually Tokyo accepted the army's action, and in February 1932 the new state of **Manchukuo** declared its independence under the protective custody of Japan's Kwantung Army. At home extremists assassinated two leaders, one a former finance minister and one an important industrialist, while ultra-nationalists praised their country's newest imperialist adventure, and the public, whipped up by newspaper accounts of army victories, praised their gallant troops and called for conservatism at home and aggressive military action abroad.

Baron Ishimoto was firmly in the jingoist camp. As he left his family once again, he explained the necessity of Japan's conquest. "America and the Soviet Union are so much larger than my country and they are rich in natural resources. Japan is a narrow land with few material resources. Consequently we can't become a great country within our own boundaries. We must develop Manchuria and Mongolia economically, and so I am going off to construct a Utopia in Manchuria." Shidzue, he insisted, should feel honored to serve the family at home while he served the nation abroad. He implied that while he was an independent man, his wife was his vassal and that of his family and country, as well.

Shidzue could not in good conscience support Keikichi's politics at home or abroad. In her 1948 autobiography she explained, "His activities had created a great gulf between us. . . . My husband had made a 180-degree conversion from his position as an intellectual humanist and pacifist and had embraced the theory that it was natural for Japan to undertake imperialist aggression in Manchuria and Mongolia. He felt that his private life should not interfere and confuse this situation. He considered this a way to make a living while aiding Japan's national policy of opening up new lands. He would not look back to his home."

The years 1930–1932 were a time of great economic hardship and emotional pain, and Shidzue was distressed about her household and her husband. Only by borrowing a little money from her father and a bank did she manage to keep her family going. Once her father rescued her from creditors who threatened to carry off the family's art treasures to pay for yet another debt her husband had incurred. Sympathy from her mother was hard to come by. She reminded Shidzue of her role as the wife in a noble family and of the responsibilities she was expected to fulfill. "My mother did not believe in consolation. She just said that women received a cruel stick. Because Mother had not known hardships she absolutely did not understand the lives of women who must confront economic problems and loss of property. She simply wondered why her daughter was grumbling. . . . There was no one but myself to rely on. I had to manage everything alone. I did not have time to stream with tears. My spirit died."

Shidzue knew the kind of behavior expected of an upper-class Japanese wife, but she had internalized a different ideal about the relationship between a husband and a wife. She was greatly influenced by Margaret Sanger and her English lover Havelock Ellis, both of whom wrote on male/female equality, sexual fulfillment, and free love. Shidzue believed that "serious relationships of couples must be absolutely bound by both respect and love. And of these the loss of respect is fatal to the couple's relationship. Consequently, it is not possible at all to save a relationship which has lost both respect and love." Her inevitable conclusion, then, was that her marriage had failed. Keikichi accepted this and gave her permission to seek a divorce.

Unfortunately the custom governing those in the upper ranks of society and Japanese family law under the Meiji Civil Code of 1898 made divorce impossible. "I was just the wife and mother and had no rights of my own," she commented in 1978. In fact, had she been able to obtain the divorce, her sons would have remained with her husband's family and she could not have expected a financial settlement. These facts were of little importance, however, as she was unable to secure the necessary permission from any two relatives among father, brothers, or brothers-in-law. Also, her husband's family opposed a divorce. "And so," she lamented, "while Ishimoto disappeared abroad, I was reproved at home." Although prevented from legally divorcing her husband of seventeen years Shidzue initiated an exchange of letters with Keikichi that resulted to her satisfaction in an informal agreement of the dissolution of their marriage. From that time on, she considered her marriage to the reactionary, tyrannical baron ended, and she accepted responsibility for her own support and for that of her sons, Arata, fourteen, and Tamio, thirteen.

A New Love

In this time of personal trial Shidzue's intensified work with the birth-control movement, and her continued participation in the **Women's Suffrage League's** campaign for women's rights provided her with some sense of intellectual and social satisfaction. The public activities, however, could not fill the void created by a loveless marriage. The longer she was alone the more acutely she became aware of her loss of male companionship and love. Though she tried to fill her lonely evenings reading love poems from the Japanese literary classic, the *Manyoshû*, romantic stories by contemporary Japanese authors, and Western novels such as *Lady Chatterley's Lover* by D. H. Lawrence, this proved inadequate. In March 1931 Shidzue turned 34.

Fortunately, that fall Shidzue once again experienced love, and thus was able to create some balance between her private and public lives. Although her new liaison complicated her existence because of the secrecy it demanded, it gave her the emotional fulfillment she needed to survive. In the prologue to her diary of 1937–1939 she wrote, "October 22, 1931 was a memorable day. It was the day in which I announced my separation from an anguished life and a history of tears. Accordingly I changed from a life of self-sacrificing devotion and began anew to receive passionate love. It was a powerful resurrection. From that time on I grew in pride day by day. Shidzue has become a fortunate woman." On this date Shidzue, still the wife of the absent Baron Ishimoto Keikichi and responsible for their sons, and Katô Kanjû, who lived with his wife Kimi, his son Nobuyuki and daughter Sumiko, determined to ignore adultery laws and family and class sensibilities in favor of personal desire.

Shidzue had known Kanjû since she and her husband returned from America in 1920. At that time Katô Kanjû often visited the Ishimoto home, for he and Keikichi shared an interest in the labor and birth-control movements. Shidzue reminisced many years later that she had felt warmly toward Kanjû, finding him a reliable man in contrast with her husband. It is not surprising, then, in the lonely and conflicted atmosphere of 1931 Shidzue permitted her association with a man whom she enjoyed and respected to grow intimate.

After Shidzue's abandonment by her husband, Kanjû became a frequent visitor to her house. She revealed years later that his presence had a calming effect. "He brought a warmth to the family just at the point when we were snapping." She then contrasted her husband's coldness and uncaring attitude toward her and their sons with the concern Katô showed all three of them. Reflecting on the world beyond her household she said, "I believe that Katô understood the pain and hardship that people suffer." Here was a man with whom she could share both her love and her vision for a just society. As Katô spent more evenings in the household, he became a part of Shidzue's family while still maintaining the headship of his legal family.

Lecturing in America

Ishimoto Shidzue's successful return to birth-control advocacy and her intimate relationship with Katô Kanjû did not solve her practical problems. Theoretically she knew her most pressing need was to become economically independent. To be truly liberated, she explained, "I had to become a working woman." She continued that because of her "experiences with the painful workings of the family system, the feudalistic discrimination against wives, and with an irresponsible husband," during her younger years, she had studied theories "about the emancipation of women and about socialism." She discovered, however, that it was not easy to convert intellectual theories into cash to pay the bills.

Late in 1931, an avenue for financial independence suddenly appeared in the form of a letter from Uncle Tsurumi Yûsuke, who was once again in New York City. He suggested that Shidzue follow his example and come to America to earn money on the lecture circuit. In the next mail she received an offer of prepayment of travel, daily expenses, and a stipend from the Feakins Lecture Bureau. She accepted and hurriedly began writing speeches and translating them into English. Shidzue had no difficulty booking passage on a ship bound for California, but getting a passport was more complicated. She explained, "Because I was the wife of a baron from a noble family, I could not leave my country without my husband's written permission. . . . In those days a wife had absolutely no freedom of travel." Shidzue had to write to the baron's last known address in Manchuria to request his written permission so that she could obtain the passport necessary to begin her journey. Though worried that she might not receive a reply in time, she made the necessary preparations of recording her plans in the official **family register** in accordance with the law, and finding an older woman to look after her teenage sons. Her husband's permission arrived just in time for her to make the booked sailing on September 28.

Shidzue arrived in San Francisco on October 14, 1932, and spent almost a full year in America, the last three months of which she spent studying at the Margaret Sanger Clinic. Her lecture tour took her to cities in California, to New York City, Boston, Palm Beach, and Dallas, several cities in between, and a few in Canada. She spoke at churches and synagogues, lecture halls, and over the radio. She had developed lectures on three topics: "The Japanese Aesthetic Sense," "The Birth Control Movement in Japan," and "The Women's Liberation Movement." At the close of each formal lecture her audiences were permitted to ask questions on any topic, and they did so enthusiastically. Often people asked about Japan's conquest of Manchuria, sometimes in a hostile manner. Consequently Shidzue found herself forced to speak on Japan's imperialist actions as frequently as on her prepared subjects. It was a trying experience both because of the anti-Japan and even anti-Japanese attitudes she encountered, and because of the strain of discussing such complex issues in English.

Shidzue had been adamantly opposed to Japan's militaristic advances in the early 1930s. She had feared what she saw as fascist-thinking national policies. Her activities for social causes, her knowledge of electoral politics through her associations with Katô Kanjû and others on the political left, and her work in the women's suffrage movement had all led her to embrace a liberal perspective. The outlawing of the Communist Party in 1928 and the mass arrests that followed, the rise of the ultra-nationalists in 1928–1932, and the public popularity of militarist actions in Manchuria had made her apprehensive about the political road the government was taking. Just the same, in America she was circumspect about her public criticism of government actions. She hedged her position by carefully addressing American concerns about Japanese foreign policy while not entangling herself in a battle with her own government.

In one often repeated critique of Japan's Manchurian policy, Shidzue said, "Overcrowding causes imperialism and imperialism causes war. The solution to overcrowding, and therefore to war, is reduction of the birth rate. Even in the case of my own country, I believe birth control is a better answer to the Manchurian problem than either emigration or imperialistic expansion." On the other hand, when a reporter asked how Japanese women felt about Japan's withdrawal from the League of Nations over its criticism of the Manchuria takeover, the baroness argued, "As long as England has India and the United States has the Philippines and other countries have outside territory, we think Japan has a right to have Manchuria." Speaking diplomatically during a time of deteriorating relations between the United States and Japan was not easy.

There is little doubt that the baroness was much more comfortable talking about Japan's feudal family system, the progressive activities of Japanese feminists, her own social activism, the birth-control movement, and the artistic accomplishments of Japanese women. But it was the subservient, soft-spoken Japanese woman in a kimono that the Americans wanted to hear about. In reviews of her lectures, "the diminutive Baroness" was described as "gentle, soft voiced, and assured, with the poise of generations of Oriental aristocrats," or "a captivating little Japanese aristocrat." In March, *Vogue* published Shidzue's article, "Kimono Into Décolleté," which teased the Western stereotypical pictures by quietly moving back and forth between Japanese women's traditional culture and that adapted from the West. Shidzue described the artistic accomplishments of the sophisticated, well-mannered and well-dressed upper-class Japanese woman. In a word, herself. In deference to American sensibilities she also painted an ideal canvas of a benevolent Japan, devoid of political conflict, but filled with the charm of the old and the comfort of the Western new. She moved in travelogue fashion from the "kimono as a work of art" to creative and fashionable Western dress, from the "national passion" for flower arrangement to the leisure activities of tennis and golf, from the celebrated art of Kabuki theater to "the movies which give [a woman] the rest and forgetfulness she craves." Even when she spoke of the "ancient and unalterable tradition of family" she managed a little joke. Describing the "utmost deference" which a woman owes her family within which "the man is the undisputed lord," she suggested, "Very often Americans, struck by the complete absence of the dreaded 'middle-age spread' in Japan, ask why a Japanese lady never gets stout. She will tell you the secret: 'Bow to your husband frequently—you will get real exercise.' Would this be a popular way of reducing in America?" Shidzue played with her role as a visiting Japanese aristocrat during her tour of America and, in the process, concealed her pain as an oppressed wife.

Shidzue, a modern woman, preferred Western clothes, but her audiences and friends loved the traditional Japanese look, and so she always wore a kimono. She considered this attire confining and uncomfortable and found it contradictory that Western feminists praised a costume which she thought represented the subjugation of Japanese women. The liberated Shidzue spent her off-duty hours shopping for more comfortable Western fashions that would form the core of her wardrobe for years to come.

Dinners, cocktail parties, and teas frequently held in her honor were a welcome relief. Although Shidzue had grown up in an atmosphere of upper-class wealth and culture, her current milieu reflected both her personal lack of funds and her nation's economic depression. Her taste for beautiful surroundings and elegant parties had not been diminished, however, by either her reduced circumstances or her liberal activism. It was luxurious to be able to forget penny-pinching and freely enjoy the splendor of lavish entertainment provided by a social elite who preferred elegance to intense political exchange.

New Projects

During Shidzue's stay in New York, she was invited by Mary Beard to her Manhattan apartment. When it came time for Shidzue to return to her hotel, Beard walked with her. For two hours these two discussed the status of contemporary Japanese women. Beard had spent much of her life writing and speaking on women's historical roles and devising a world-encompassing theory on that subject. If only there were a book that showed just how Japanese women fit into her scheme, she remarked. Suddenly she turned to her Japanese guest and exclaimed that she should write such a book, her life story. While Shidzue demurred at first, she soon saw it as an opportunity to expose the family system that had exploited her and all women, and the lordly manner of Japanese husbands. It could be both a personal history and a handbook for securing women's rights. She would do it!

During the next two years Shidzue focused much of her intellectual efforts on her autobiography. She worked sixteen hours a day for almost a year. First she completed a Japanese version, then laboriously translated that into English. When she finally mailed off the finished manuscript, she felt as if she had given birth. More than just Shidzue's life story, it was, as well, a contemporary account of women's difficulties under a feudal family system. In August 1935 *Facing Two Ways: The Story of My Life,* was published simultaneously in the United States, England, and Sweden. When the book appeared the *Mainichi Newspaper* commented, "A Japanese woman writer has become a best seller. Regardless of what one thinks of the text, Ishimoto Shidzue's *Facing Two Ways* is having an extremely promising sale." In fact the content was so controversial that a Japanese translation had to wait another fifty years.

During this same period, Shidzue reconstituted her birth-control organization toward more effective advocacy based on what she had learned at Sanger's clinic in New York. In the fall and winter of 1933–1934, she helped to form the **Women's Birth Control League of Japan,** which opened information bureaus in hospitals in four villages. Shidzue also wrote articles for women's columns in newspapers trying to generate nationwide interest in the practice of birth control. She was quite successful, for she received more than a thousand letters within the first six months from women who had questions ranging from contraceptive choice to how to care for their children during illness.

Shidzue recognized the political nature of her clinic work and connected birth control with women's liberation from **feudalism.** "I was saddened by the tired and unhealthy appearances of the women [in the hospitals]," she wrote in 1948, "and by the fact that they seemed to have so little time off between pregnancies. . . . I believed that the distress of these women could not be solved without social liberation from the feudal yoke and economic pressures they experienced. Although I believed it was important to understand this fundamental truth, I also felt that the practical knowledge of birth control would improve the welfare of these women on a daily basis and would save them as individuals." Armed with this perspective, on March 1, 1934, Shidzue and a few members of the Women's Birth Control League of Japan opened a birth-control clinic.

Shidzue explained her clinic role as educational. She would lecture to groups of women on birth-control methods. "As an introductory lesson to teach contraceptive methods to sexually ignorant women I used a model of the female reproductive organs which I brought back from America. With this model, which was a dissection of the reproductive organs cut away in such a manner that you could have both an internal and external view, the women were able to understand the process of conception. Thus I was able to introduce them to birth-control methods and I could teach them about the variety of contraceptive methods available." After her lecture each woman would speak individually with a physician to work out a plan for the contraceptive method that would most effectively meet her needs.

In letters to friends abroad Shidzue lamented the end of her American freedom. "It has been very hard for me to adjust myself again to this conservative and reactionary country after spending the most delightful months in a democratic country mingling among the most progressive people." She also commented on her larger worries brought on by her government's actions at home and abroad. "It is hard at present to promote any progressive movement as we are in what they call an extraordinary moment anticipating serious international problems. . . . However, birth control is needed with acuteness whether the authorities believe in it or not."

Shidzue found it wearying to be continuously battling the authorities as she fought for her right to provide clinic facilities and educational materials on family planning. Her determination, however, was strong and her belief in the importance of the right of women to plan their families and the larger cause of women's right to be equal with men kept her jousting with all levels of governmental power. Both political freedom and reproductive freedom were tied to Shidzue's concept of liberation for women within a democratic society. Both ideas were bound to get her in trouble as a kind of fascism tightened its hold on Japan.

Borderline Activities

In the winter of 1935 Katô Kanjû was invited by a committee of the American Federation of Labor to visit the United States on a fact-finding and speaking tour. Since his English was minimal, and he had never visited the United States before, he relied on Shidzue for practical help. The speeches they prepared emphasized the importance of securing international opposition to Japan's imperialist actions in China and urged formation of a united international labor movement opposed to worldwide war.

Speaking to about five hundred people in Manhattan, Katô warned that a war spirit had been nurtured by Japanese imperialists and that the hostilities could spread and eventually involve America. He spoke of countering militarist and capitalist efforts to win over the workers to the side of the imperialist classes. Japanese labor, he insisted, opposed the war and sought bonds of friendship with American workers. In America Katô felt free to speak as a political radical, but what he said from this podium was no different from what he had been writing in Japanese journals.

Katô returned to Japan on September 5 and began working for a "**popular front**." Just that summer communist leaders from around the world had met in Moscow for the Seventh Comintern Meeting. This international group of communists had agreed on a wartime strategy of forming a popular front with other parties to their right, most particularly the socialists. This would be especially important for parties in France and Spain and other parts of Europe where socialists and communists were continuously fighting for labor's support and where pressure from fascism was at its strongest. The Japanese representative at this meeting was the radical Communist Party exile Nosaka Sanzô, living at that time with Mao's Communist Chinese in Hunan, China. Katô had just met secretly with Nosaka in New York City where the two men agreed that Katô would lead his socialist following into a popular front.

By January 1936, the political left in Japan was excited about a socialist-led, democratic future for Japan. Unfortunately, on **February 26th,** right-wing lower-level military officers attempted a coup against the government. The next day martial law was declared and the insurgents capitulated. Although this event seemed to forecast a future of greater repression for Japan, social activists like Kanjû and Shidzue saw it as merely a setback. In fact, it marked a successful moment in Shidzue's campaign for social and political freedom. In the midst of the turmoil, Margaret Sanger, who was on her way home from India, docked briefly in Tokyo. As Shidzue casually commented in a letter, "Tokyo was then and is still under martial law, and no public meeting was permitted, but she [Sanger] had no trouble landing in Yokohama . . ." Rather, the problem the women faced was that martial law prevented public rallies. This time it wasn't Sanger or her birth-control message that the government feared, but rather the possibility of public disorder created by crowds. In fact, in private meetings and through extensive newspaper coverage, Sanger's visit did much to publicize Ishimoto's birth control activities.

Ishimoto Shidzue and Margaret Sanger in Tokyo February 1936, shortly after martial law had been declared. Courtesy of the Sophia Smith Collection, Smith College. Reprinted with permission.

A Secret Liaison

During the thirties, until their arrest in December 1937, Shidzue and Kanjû publicly supported each other's political activities. Secretly, they enjoyed an intimate personal relationship. Kanjû invited Shidzue to join him in his quest to undo the imperialist actions of the nationalist/militarist, or as he preferred to call it, "fascist," government. Shidzue eagerly accepted. She had opposed the government's foreign policy beginning with the Manchurian Incident, and found government domestic policy anathema in its oppression of women. Sharing Kanjû's platform offered important public exposure for advocacy of family planning and women's liberation. Changes in Article Five of the Peace Preservation Law promulgated in 1922 had given women the right to gather for political purposes, but, even among socialists, patriarchal custom would prevent her from participating in party deliberations. In describing her relationship with Kanjû during the thirties, Shidzue emphasized their mutual political interests, saying that while Kanjû struggled for an independent political base, the two of them had had many opportunities for "intimate relations." These included "instruction from him in matters of political combat and questions of social concern."

In an interview in 1983 Shidzue remembered these years somewhat less romantically. The interviewer questioned her bluntly about her relationship with Katô Kanjû during the mid-thirties. Hadn't she "kept company" with Kanjû in spite of the fact that her divorce plans could not be realized, and couldn't this be labeled "free love"? No, she responded, it could not be called free love. The two of them were "circumspect" in their relationship. The interviewer then asked whether Katô's wife was aware of this relationship, to which Shidzue responded that she was sure Kimi inferred what was going on, but was not sure she understood the extent of the companionship. "And didn't he have children?" "Yes." "And didn't it pain you to know that although you loved Katô he had a wife and children?" "No, I did not worry at all. In those days a man who worked in the labor movement simply, in truth, did not have any responsibilities toward women. He treated all women, whoever they were, the same." "Ah," retorted the interviewer, "In those days if men in the labor movement subjugated women. . . ." She interrupted, "Ignored. They ignored women. . . . Yes all the men were like that. Men working in the labor movement were definitely not democratic in their relations with women. It's all very painful to talk about but women were ignored."

Probing further, the interviewer commented that she had disagreed intellectually with her husband, Ishimoto Keikichi, over issues of subjugation of women and feudal standards for marriage, and had wanted a divorce. And yet, she loved Katô Kanjû without reserve and was not repelled by his apparent belief in the inferior role of women. "This is really incomprehensible," the interviewer concluded. Shidzue attempted to explain this contradiction. "Through me, for the first time, Katô met a woman of intellect." She continued, that since she had been "baptized in liberalism," she trusted the labor movement and she accepted the importance of Kanjû's leadership role. Her admiration and respect for him made it possible for her to accept his interpretation of the role of women. Her affection and esteem had become intertwined. "Ha ha. Love is blind," the interviewer blandly concluded.

Though not without substantial intellectual contradiction, her relationship with Kanjû filled the depressing void in her life. She was willing to follow him and learn from him and any elements of inequality in their relationship were irrelevant to her. Love may not have been blind, but it certainly was forgiving. Privately, she enjoyed his companionship and publicly she shared the speaker's platform with him. She loved him without reservation and believed that he returned her love as best he could. This was enough for her. She did not feel it necessary to work out the ideological inconsistencies in their relationship, or the fact that in many ways it was as unequal as her marriage had been. And so Shidzue's love of Kanjû, and her overt support of his political activities, would place her beside him, and consequently in jeopardy in December 1937.

Writing Women's History

Shidzue's successful American lecture tour and her best-selling book had only temporarily solved her financial problems. Her work in the birth-control movement and other political activities did not help economically. Kanjû was not responsible for her or her sons. Money was always tight. Therefore, when Mary Beard contacted her in the fall of 1935 with a new writing project, a history of Japanese women for a multi-volume international women's history, Shidzue accepted the task, anticipating further royalties. Fortunately she was also enticed by the assignment, for not only would there be no future financial rewards, but the project had the markings of "dangerous thoughts."

Shidzue met Beard's new challenge with great excitement and immediate action. She asked four trusted friends to join. In addition to this core of women researchers a few liberal men were invited to help. In fact it was a young professor who borrowed the library books and secured a research room for the group at Tokyo Imperial University. As Shidzue explained, "When we started this work and wanted to go to the library, we were told that no woman could cross its sacred threshold, so when we wanted reference material we had to bow to the men and beg them to look up our references."

Over the course of her research Shidzue formulated a theory suggesting that oppression of women in Japan had appeared with the privatization of property and the legal protection of inheritance by a male heir. A husband's demand that his wife's chastity be carefully guarded to ensure purity of the ancestral line led to the concept of wives as chattel. It was to ensure continuity of the family line through protection of private property that Confucian morals were imported from China, bringing women under the total control of men. The Japanese family system with a male autocratic head was superimposed on this, Shidzue concluded, to assure male supremacy and subjugate women. Shidzue believed her research showed a clear personal connection between the economics of private property and the development of a family system that had enslaved her and led her into economic depression.

Because the group's writings contradicted official histories and challenged official family law, they believed that they could be prosecuted under the dangerous thoughts provision of the 1925 Peace Preservation Law. Consequently they felt they could not meet openly. From 1935 to 1939, they concealed their activities by disguising the purpose of their meetings. Members would come to Shidzue's home as if on a casual visit and stay for research, discussion, and writing. They would also meet at an appointed restaurant or would be alerted by a cryptic, brief announcement in the personal column of the newspaper. Shidzue believed that the authorities were determined to suppress any historical research that might contradict official doctrine. As she said a decade later, "By the time we finished compiling the material, Japan was moving toward fascism and all history treating facts as such was against the national policy. Many prominent scholars were taken to court because well-indoctrinated associates accused them of writing and teaching the truth about Japanese history."

Finally, in 1939, Shidzue wrote to Mary Beard saying, simply, "It is finished." Mary was delighted that a portion of the evidence she sought in support of her own theories of women's history was completed. She ignored the fact that Shidzue had drawn conclusions that were quite the opposite of Beard's. The Japanese feminist believed she had provided evidence of patriarchal oppression of women, while the American, who rejected the concept of patriarchal domination, found the work anti-feminist in its support of women's enduring power.

A Second Lecture Tour of America

Far from bringing in additional funds to add to Shidzue's meager bank account, the women's history project consumed some of her own money. Fortunately in 1936 Shidzue was, once again, invited to lecture America. She considered this trip a financial necessity. Leaving her two grown sons, Arata now eighteen and Tamio seventeen, she set off for the West Coast arriving in Seattle on January 10, 1937. It was a grueling tour, for in addition to the constant lecturing in English and the drudgery of long-distance travel, Shidzue was often on exhibit as the guest of honor at teas and dinner parties, and was asked to speak informally with members of the American birth-control movement. This was not the romantic adventure of the first tour, it was hard work performed to earn desperately needed cash.

As she crossed the country presenting her prepared talks, Shidzue tried to balance her advocacy of birth control with her fear of agitating her government, which disapproved of limiting births. "There is no law against birth control in Japan, and no religious prejudice, but we do encounter political opposition from leaders who believe that strong soldiers are synonymous with a rich country," she explained. "My answer is that soldiers are stronger if they have grown up in families which have been able to adjust their size to their incomes." She added, "There is a great and growing demand from the masses for adequate and reliable information and any announcement of a birth-control lecture is certain to draw a very large audience."

Shidzue never equated the need for birth control with an attempt to breed out a less economically fruitful or a less desirable class of people. Her socialist ideology assured that she would see limitation of family size as a positive good in itself for mothers and for children rather than as a class weapon. This meant that in the future her perspective on family planning clashed with official government policy based on eugenics, or breeding for improvement of the race.

Misplaced Optimism by the Political Left

While Shidzue was in America, Kanjû had founded a new left-wing socialist party, the Japan Proletarian Party, which prepared to run candidates in the Diet election scheduled for April 30, 1937. When Shidzue returned from America in May 1937, she found Kanjû and other socialist friends elated over the results of this election. Although the **Proletarian Party** seated only one representative, Katô Kanjû, the less radical Social Masses Party more than doubled their representation to thirty-seven seats. It seemed to those on the left that many voters had responded positively to the yearlong campaign in journals and from platforms against what they saw as the government's rapid advance toward fascism. Criticism of the conservative parties and of government policy appeared to be bearing fruit. The April election was seen as a positive turning point for democracy in Japan.

Shidzue accepted the Proletarian Party's invitation to speak publicly at their celebratory gatherings. She was concerned about her government, which increasingly pressured women's liberation and family-planning movements, and she found hope in the only political party that held high its antiwar banner and provided room on its platform for a speaker interested in women's issues. She used this opportunity to proclaim the right of women to plan the spacing and size of their families, and to speak out for full human rights for women. She saw women as part of the proletarian have-nots and felt they should receive their due from this party dedicated to the masses. This was not a dreary task for Shidzue; it was an exhilarating mission, and in all of these activities and associations she enjoyed herself immensely. What a contrast this lecturing posed to the tour she had just completed! In America she need have no fear of the authorities, but found her reception tied closely to interest in her apparel and appearance and the exotic figure she cut. In Japan fear was ever present, but her cause was seriously accepted and the political goals were clearly vital.

Because of restrictions in force by the Home Ministry, and concerns about "dangerous thoughts" as stated in the

Peace Preservation Law, these political meetings and rallies were attended by police. It was government policy to pressure political parties through careful attention to the wording of all public utterances. When the police heard particular words, such as "military dictatorship," or "fascism," or the expression of suspicious ideas, such as implying a class separation between the "masses" and military officers, they would stop the speakers and issue warnings, cut the speaker off entirely, or, finally, remove the speaker for questioning and possible arrest.

Shidzue was a featured speaker at an election reception celebrating Kanjû's victory. After she had given her prepared remarks, she discovered that the next speaker had not yet arrived. She had no alternative but to speak extemporaneously for an additional half hour. Her wording was not as carefully restrained as it had been in her prepared text. Her delivery became agitated, and it was obvious that she had gone beyond the accepted solemn manner of presentation. The watching police shouted at her to stop, and then led her away. They detained her at the local police station until late that night. Finally, admonishing her that a housewife should not be out so late, they sent her home.

She was greeted on her return by two very frightened sons. Since the dangers for those who participated in suspicious politics were obvious to all, she could not pacify their fears. She believed, however, that they understood how important proclaiming human rights was both for her own sense of personal freedom and for women's liberation in general. This brush with the police should have warned Shidzue of difficult times ahead, but in May and June 1937 it was a minor reminder of official power. Kanjû, Shidzue, and their associates optimistically felt that liberal ideas would win the political war and Japan would be swayed from its militarist ways.

IV

Embracing Dangerous Thoughts

During the summer of 1937 the political left was surprised and alarmed, then put on guard by an incident between Japanese and Chinese troops that occurred near the Marco Polo Bridge just outside Beijing. At first the fighting seemed a minor clash that would be easily confined. In fact the incident, which escalated quickly, threatened to become a full-scale war. The warning sounded by this incident was clearly heard by those on the left. By late July Katô Kanjû and his colleagues began to tone down their opposition to Japan's China policy. It was obvious to all socialists that their freedom to criticize government action was on a short chain. Softening their post-election rhetoric, Proletarian Party spokesmen no longer used the term "fascist," spoke of Japan's leaders as military and bureaucratic "dictators," or stated direct disapproval of the government's China policy. Instead they began to talk about providing for the families of the soldiers at the front in the face of a declining standard of living for Japan's citizens.

On July 22, Prime Minister Konoe Fumimaro called a Special Diet Session. Over the next two weeks this extraordinary Diet passed several bills affecting every facet of Japan's economic life. The primary objectives were to provide for economic self-sufficiency and a strong financial base for the military in hopes of effecting a swift end to what was characterized as an "incident" in China. The Diet quickly passed thirty-four of the thirty-five bills. The nationalists and militarists had won the hour, and opposition to Japan's imperialist adventure was crumbling. Disagreement with government policy could fall under the "dangerous thoughts" clause of the 1925 Peace Preservation Act.

In China things looked very unstable. On August 9, the Japanese army in Shanghai began to make new demands on the Chinese, who responded by moving three divisions in place to attack. The Japanese army and navy fought back; Chinese aircraft bombed the Japanese; in retaliation Japanese aircraft bombed Nanjing; and on August 13, the Japanese cabinet authorized bombs to be dropped on Shanghai. The "incident" was widening. A war seemed inevitable.

On July 31, Shidzue went forward with her plans to open a new birth-control clinic, even though she recognized the risk in this decision. She also continued arrangements to welcome Margaret Sanger and her entourage, who were to stop over for a week en route to China. On August 20, Shidzue traveled to Kobe to meet her friends. By this time her panic had subsided to mild concern and her resolve increased. In spite of the escalation of the war in China she reasoned that the authorities did not have time, manpower, or adequate interest in these women or their message to halt their activities. In truth, the government officially opposed limiting births but neither the dispensing of family-planning information nor the establishment of birth-control clinics was yet illegal. They might represent a form of "dangerous thoughts" but during the summer of 1937 the Home Ministry and the **special higher police** were far too busy checking on well-known public men whose political pronouncements might stir up opposition to the escalating hostilities in China to bother with these women. Shidzue felt she could proceed with her arrangements making only minor changes to satisfy local police regulations or placate nervous lecture hall managers.

Discreet Activism

Shidzue had arranged for Margaret to lecture the day she arrived but a broken arm sent her to a hospital instead. It was Dorothy Brush who accompanied Shidzue to Ama-no-Hashidate, a small town on the Japan Sea about five hours by train from Kobe. After dropping off their suitcases at the inn, they went to the local police station for the obligatory entry of their names into local government and military records. Dorothy was also asked to show her speech. To her surprise the police assured her that she could speak freely about birth control, but she was warned not to mention anything about the "little difficulty" with China.

That evening the two women were brought to a large hall lined with individual knee-high tables. Seated behind each table on the tatami flooring was a kimono-clad Japanese, only three or four of whom were women. Policemen lined the sliding doors. When invited, Dorothy stood in stockinged feet and give her address with Shidzue interpreting. Brush had brought films showing the human biology of reproduction and explaining the use of contraceptives. Before showing the films she requested that anyone who was not a physician leave, a required procedure in America. She was taken aback when Shidzue, the policemen, and everyone else laughed heartily. Why should some adults be prevented from viewing an informational film? In America such shocking pictures were not permitted to be shown publicly to anyone outside the medical profession. In Japan they were shown to all.

By the time Ishimoto and Brush joined Sanger in Tokyo, she felt well enough to carry out her heavy schedule. Shidzue arranged formal lectures for physicians, birth-control advocates, Tokyo municipal leaders, and social activists. She also set up informal gatherings that progressive men and women—writers, poets, doctors, and labor leaders—attended. At no time did the group have difficulty with the police or the military. The government appeared to consider this example of "dangerous thoughts" minor compared with its obsessive concern about the "**China Incident.**" The women were permitted to say what they wanted about women's issues but were not even to speak privately about the "chastisement" of China.

Geisha and Prostitutes

Although most days were filled with lectures and discussions, on the first free evening Sanger asked to visit a **geisha.** Shidzue arranged such an interview at an expensive tea house with a young woman in her twenties who spoke English well. She told Sanger that she had graduated from a Kyoto girls college and had become a geisha in order to support her mother and grandmother. She expected to complete her four-year contract in one more year and would then learn stenography and find another job. She had been attracted to the geisha world by the artistic accomplishments these women displayed. She seemed anxious to dispel the stereotype of geisha as lovers and prostitutes.

The next evening Baroness Ishimoto picked up Sanger and Brush at their hotel in her chauffeur-driven car and they set off for the infamous **Yoshiwara District.** Brush asked her what the chauffeur thought about this trip. "The Baroness replied with a smile that he was not paid to think. Shidzue then described the role of licensed prostitution in Japan. She emphasized the financial gain for the government from high taxes, frequent health examinations, and close police supervision. All of this was designed to protect the men. 'But what happens if they [the prostitutes] do contract venereal disease?' asked Margaret. 'They are thrown out—turned over to the unlicensed unregulated section. You'll see them there, if you still have the courage to go.'"

Entering one of the legal houses, Margaret asked to interview a prostitute. Shidzue arranged a meeting in the "Madam's" presence. They learned from the "Madam" that the young girl earned "not one yen until she has repaid all she has cost us." According to the rate card in the room her charge was "about seventy-five American cents for an hour; two dollars for an afternoon; four dollars for a whole night."

Shidzue directed the chauffeur to drive from the Yoshiwara to the unlicensed quarters. This visit turned out to be a frightening experience. The group left a broad avenue and drove down dark, winding, crowded streets which seemed like alleys to the Americans. There were no protective police here. It was an area which did not welcome foreign guests or a seemingly wealthy Japanese woman. The three women actually got out of the car expecting to survey the area on foot, but a shower of stones and angry shouts soon sent them scurrying back inside. A man grabbed Shidzue roughly by the arm and growled something at her. Within the safety of the car, which quickly sped off to the main road, Shidzue told her friends that the angry man demanded to know why she would show these awful sights to Westerners. Others were calling out taunts of "Is it me you want?" and "Haven't we met before girlies?"

Brush and Sanger saw the world as full of social and economic evils caused primarily by overpopulation, and they saw birth control as the solution. Moreover, the Americans did not credit the elite activists who had been their primary examples of Japanese women as much more liberated than the women in the **"water trades"** they had just visited. Although Ishimoto took them to wealthy homes where they were lavishly entertained, introduced them to the cream of the artistic and educated Tokyo society, and arranged discussions with politically conscious women, Sanger and Brush believed that few Japanese women would ever break the bonds of female subservience.

Celebrating a New Clinic

Shidzue decided that in spite of the politically dangerous times, she would hold a reception that would both honor her guests and celebrate the establishment of her new private clinic. The festivities of August 30 began with Shidzue's opening remarks in which she praised her own group's progress. In just three short years the Women's Birth Control League of Japan had been consulted in person or by letter by more than ten thousand women. "The income of most of these women's husbands is 30 yen (about $10.00) a month, and they have families averaging 6 and 8 children." The desire for birth-control information was strong but the ability to pay was minimal. She then commented that because of militarist policies they could not openly solicit funds to help these poor women.

Margaret Sanger's comments were brief, cordial, and particularly laudatory of her colleague and host, Ishimoto Shidzue. She placed her alongside Mary Wollstonecraft, Madame Curie, Susan B. Anthony, Olive Schreiner, and Ellen Key in an international pantheon of those pioneering for women's rights. The reception was a great success and a memorable occasion for Margaret, who left Japan on September 3 aboard the bombed and crippled S.S. *President Hoover.* The ship's "riddled deck" and "shattered glass" echoed "the tragic and harrowing conditions in China." Shidzue was left with memories of the brief but exciting visit, in which she and the Americans pledged a common bond of friendship. Within four months the Americans would read of Shidzue's arrest.

Destruction of the Left

The war news worsened in September, and the government became even less tolerant of "dangerous thoughts." Although Shidzue was aware that she was engaging in suspicious activities, she did not slow her efforts to provide birth-control materials. She requested and received supplies from America, and spoke with doctors about experiments with new forms of contraceptives. She found the process of simply getting and distributing her supplies more complicated and expensive, and yet she managed successfully to ignore tightened rules, and avoid payment or, if necessary, pay for added import taxes. She found substitute materials for those in scarce supply due to increased military requirements. Her work was much harder but her efforts were rewarded many times over through letters she received from grateful women.

In the government, military and bureaucratic power forcibly united all Diet members in support of their China policy. On September 9, the 72nd Diet was called into special session to legislate additional money for financing the war in China. The government continued to proclaim that the fighting constituted a quick clean-up effort and that the China Incident would be resolved with just a few more troops and the 2.2 billion yen appropriation which it was requesting. Political cooperation was expected, and Prime Minister Konoe was pleased with the unanimous patriotic response. The special appropriations of the 71st (July) and 72nd (September) Diet sessions combined to almost double the budget for 1937–1938. Nationalism and xenophobia seemed to catch hold of everyone in power; there was no room for public opposition to these wartime demands for increased military requirements.

By November 1, public statements against government policy in China constituted "dangerous thoughts" and were punishable under the Peace Preservation Law. Furthermore, the legislation passed in the two special Diet sessions, and supported by all parties, left and right, empowered the government to requisition all or parts of factories for war use, to order the distribution or supply of raw materials, and to make any other centralized decision deemed necessary to carry out its national and international missions. By November 30, a secret Home Ministry document claimed that the political left was no longer a threat on the China issue. Katô Kanjû's party, along with other socialist parties, had capitulated.

As the chairman of the party, Katô Kanjû left Japan for the war zone December 2, on an obligatory trip to "**comfort the troops.**" The government expected someone in each political party and all other national organizations to perform this duty. Had Katô's party not sent someone to the front, their patriotism would have been questioned and their already tenuous existence further jeopardized.

On December 13, the Japanese forces capped two months of bloody military battles and wanton killing of civilians with a victorious entry into the Chinese Nationalist government's capital city, Nanjing. On that day it seemed as if the Japanese army had finally achieved a victory that would force negotiations to end the war. In fact the Konoe government discovered that it was no closer to an end to hostilities than just after the Marco Polo Incident in July. On December 14, an even more despotic Home Minister was appointed from the highest ranks of the military. Elimination of the left wing was only one day off.

The Arrests

At six o'clock on the morning of December 15, 1937, Shidzue was awakened from a sound sleep by the excited voice of her maid, Sendai, who was yelling to someone outside. "*Dame desu, dame desu, Okusama* will not let you come in! You can't do this without my mistress' permission." Shidzue, who could not quite hear what the intruder was saying, got up, quickly wrapped something around her, and went toward the front door where she saw three men. Sendai turned to her and said, "Okusama, the police have forced their way in." Shidzue recalled that

Standing left to right Sendai, the maid, Arata, Shidzue, Tamio.
Courtesy of Katô Shidzue.

moment. "In the twinkling of an eye my sleepy head had cleared and my heart called out, 'they've come.'" In those few seconds she vacillated between thinking she should fight this intrusion and rejoicing that what she feared for so long had finally come to pass.

One of the men handed her a paper and another told her to hurry up and get dressed. She was under arrest. Having heard many stories from communists about the stark, unheated jails, Shidzue dressed in kimono, a wool sweater, and camel hair coat in preparation for the discomfort of a cell. She also packed as much warm, padded silk clothing, from long underwear to jacket, that a small suitcase would hold. Then she combed her hair, washed, and put on her makeup in preparation for her ordeal to come. This took the twenty minutes she had requested from the police.

On December 15, at six A.M. four hundred and seventy-three people were rounded up by local police and special higher police from the Home Ministry and taken to local police stations for questioning. At five P.M. Katô Kanjû was arrested just as his ship docked at Nagasaki and was taken to Roppongi police station in Tokyo. The efficient execution of the operation meant the raids had been carefully planned.

The public learned of these arrests on December 22, after the police lifted a press ban. Articles featured Katô Kanjû and three other prominent leaders who were in custody. Front-page coverage was also accorded the only two women arrested, Ishimoto Shidzue, identified as a propagandist for Margaret Sanger's birth-control movement, and Hirabayashi Taiko, a well-known proletarian writer. The front page of *Asahi Newspaper* referred to the two women as roses in the midst of thorns. Another newspaper called them "two red flowers" (communists) of the "Popular Front." Baroness Ishimoto was featured in articles in *The New York Times, The New York Herald Tribune,* and *The Christian Science Monitor* as well.

Many of those arrested, like Ishimoto Shidzue, were held for a brief time and then released with warnings not to participate in political activities, publish, or speak publicly. Others were detained in local jails for lengthy periods of time, and either tried and released or sentenced to imprisonment. For those detained and/or sentenced, the average imprisonment was two to three years. Katô Kanjû was sentenced to three years and actually served two full years, after which he remained under surveillance until the end of the war. Hirabayashi Taiko received a sentence of several years. She was released after serving eight months because she had contracted tuberculosis, which was aggravated by the damp, unheated prison cell.

No one was executed under the Peace Preservation Law, and it was primarily communists who remained in jail until the victorious American military freed political prisoners in 1945. Both the Justice Department and the Home Ministry had roles in prosecuting "thought" criminals, those who opposed the war in China and, later, militarist policies in general. Though the Justice Department was the harsher in its application of the laws, both ministries made at least a show of following written legal procedures, used the court system in place, and did not set up a separate prison system. There were abuses of justice including torture and incarceration without trial or sentencing, but most "thought" criminals simply experienced the harsh prison conditions and abuse of civil liberties that were the lot of all Japanese caught in the criminal justice system.

There were no concentration camps and no policies of racial or ethnic annihilation, though Koreans often received harsher treatment within the prison system in general. Arrest by the special higher police was more feared than by local police. Seizure by the military police (*Kempeitai*) was the most terrifying of all. Just the same, in spite of the deification of the emperor, Japan did not have an all-powerful leader like Hitler or Stalin, and did not have a single, all-powerful party like the Nazi Party in Germany, the Fascists in Italy, or the Communist Party in the USSR. As bad as the special higher police, and even military police within Japan, might seem, they were not comparable to the German SS and the Gestapo, or the Checka in the USSR. The Japanese authorities worked toward reformation of wayward citizens, and conversion of anti-militarists to conformity with national policies. This was called *tenkô*. If that could be achieved, the converted "thought" criminal became an ally of the government and was released. Many leftists converted without experiencing prison at all and proved their worth by aiding their new allies.

Jail and Interrogation

After the police searched her house, they drove their prisoner, the Baroness Ishimoto Shidzue, to her local police station, a dreary place with bare floors, no heat, and cramped rooms. She was not taken immediately to a cell, but was ushered into an office in which three members of the special higher police were eating lunch. For more than three hours during this first afternoon's interrogation, Shidzue suffered equal parts of pain and insult; not physical pain, but the pain of humiliation and distress. During the interrogation the police displayed literary works, labor newspapers, magazine articles, and campaign speeches by both Kanjû and Shidzue. They even produced some of Shidzue's English writings and asked that she explain them.

The interrogation was interrupted by a phone call, and Shidzue heard one of the three say, "Ha—We don't have any proof yet, but we are investigating these communications one by one. Yes, yes—until four P.M." This was the only hint she had about what was going on. Much of what followed consisted of insults. They made such comments as; "These are either stupid or clever," in reference to personal letters from Katô; "I would rather a woman have seven pregnancies," in reference to her propagation of birth-control education; and "Even if your husband were to return to Tokyo he would have to sleep in the Station Hotel because he couldn't get into your house," an apparent indication that Ishimoto Keikichi was no longer welcome in his wife's home. Shidzue was pained by their arrogant manner but remained polite.

After several hours of interrogation she was taken to her cell. Since this was a neighborhood jail it had few cells. A variety of criminals, some held for theft, some for fraud, and so forth, were all thrown in together. The first cell held about thirty men. They all stared at her. This, thankfully, was not where they would put her. She was to stay in a small three-mat room (6' × 9') with barred windows, which was set aside for women prisoners. It was already occupied by another woman, who, she later learned, was about twenty-eight and had been arrested for some sex-related offense. At night these two women were joined by the jail's maid. Shidzue mused that even though the maid had committed no crime, she, too, was incarcerated.

Shidzue was devastated by her circumstances, and called

on Kanjû, her inner strength, to help her to endure the ordeal "as a soldier of humanity" so that "together with you [Kanjû] I will understand both suffering and joy." She was not permitted to have any books nor allowed to write. She did nothing but think while she fought the urge to cry. Her first meal was brought to her in a dirty wooden bowl. Even though it smelled awful, and was served with just a cup of hot water as accompaniment, she ate it, for she realized that it was important for "a fighter" to fill her stomach. Her cellmate doubled over after eating the food, saying her belly ached and that she was cold. She then asked Shidzue if she played *mah jongg* and when she was told no, suggested that Shidzue was probably above such card games. Even in prison Shidzue's upper-class status was evident.

The Baroness Ishimoto was formally interrogated on December 18 by three members of the special higher police from headquarters, the dreaded "thought police" who uncovered crimes against the 1925 Peace Preservation Law. Shidzue was brought to a special room, where she was arbitrarily ordered first to stand and then to sit. Her interrogators sat in front of her at a large table. Recognizing the significance of this meeting, she had dressed herself in *kimono* and **haori** and had taken great pains combing her hair, a difficult task, for her hair ornaments had been taken away on the first day.

"Do you know why you've been brought here and did you consent?" one began. The prisoner answered that she had been shown a summons that said it was because Katô Kanjû was under suspicion of violation of the Peace Preservation Law. The police had linked her to the popular front through her proven association with Katô. They scolded her, a woman of high social standing, for joining such people. It was even more shameful, they said, that she had criticized her own government in a foreign country (the United States). She replied that her lecture tours were a people-to-people exchange and such international mingling represented hope for the future of all humanity. She thought to herself, "Your [Kanjû's] words streamed through my breast. My victory would be like that of a *sumo* wrestler who, though lighter in weight, would use spiritual strength to overcome the heavier opponent."

Her interrogations, though frequent, were not continuous. The content ran the gamut of topics from politics; the popular front movement, the Proletarian Party, Katô Kanjû; to her own social activism; the birth-control movement, political rights for women, social equality for women. Her interrogators asked her if she advocated birth control for anti-militarist reasons. She explained that it was for the sake of poor mothers who could not afford to have more children. They criticized her work in this movement saying it was contrary to national requirements during the present emergency. She argued for birth-control education in order to protect mothers and to reduce the high rate of infant mortality. The inquisitors were concerned about the danger of her movement to the national polity (*kokutai*). By associating her movement with the words "dangerous to the **kokutai**" the police appeared to be laying the groundwork for her imprisonment under the 1925 Peace Preservation Law. She reminded them, "Aren't thoughts about women's liberation and birth control legal? Please instruct me in the ways in which these can be considered crimes. . . . If I have made a mistake I will admit it. Just tell me my mistake, what I have done wrong."

Questioning turned to the government's China policy and Shidzue's attitudes about the effect military actions might have on the home front. She responded that the war was costing a lot of money and would cause economic distress for everyone. She concluded that the economic consequences of the war would be devastating for all citizens regardless of the morality of the war in China. This line of questioning was directed at two dangerous issues. First, Shidzue seemed to link large numbers of children with the problems of poverty and suggested that birth control, a practice currently opposed by the government, was the solution. Second, the focus on the impoverishment of the working class grew out of the Proletarian Party's July public-policy statement about the welfare of military families and the party's intention to assist soldiers returning home. The authorities were leading Shidzue toward admissions which would firmly tie her to Kanjû and to the antiwar position they ascribed to his Proletarian Party.

The regimentation of jail life impressed Shidzue. She was told when to eat, when to go to bed, when to get up. She was ordered to and from interrogation sessions at which she was told when and where to stand or sit. Her meals were served three times a day at exact hours in a corner of the women's cell. For the most part they consisted of "foreign" (bad) rice, two *takuwan* (pickled radish), and scraps of boiled vegetables for lunch, the same for dinner plus *misô* soup and, on occasion, a small chop. She could not have books or writing materials and was not supposed to talk with her cellmate or the maid. When she was not eating, sleeping, or being interrogated, she had little to do but think.

Once, on December 24, the routine was broken by a visit from two doctors making routine examinations of all the prisoners. Prison officials were concerned about "cement illnesses," such as kidney problems, scabby skin, and other skin diseases. After looking at the men in the neighboring cell, they came to her without even washing their hands, and expected her to disrobe and let them examine her body while the crowd of men looked on. "To even suggest such a thing in that cold, damp, unclean and public atmosphere was contemptuous," she exclaimed to her diary, and so she adamantly refused to comply. In the end the soft-spoken one merely looked at her face while not touching her body, and said, "That's fine."

She was permitted to have visitors with the police present and members of her family came regularly. One of Shidzue's most welcome visitors was her uncle, Tsurumi Yûsuke. He had asked government officials the reason for his niece's arrest. Tsurumi, a respected member of the centrist **Popular Government Party,** was informed that her association with the popular front had made her suspect. In the days to come her close relationship with Uncle Yûsuke, the fact that her brother Hirota Yôji was a diplomat, and her relationship with the Ishimoto family helped to balance Shidzue's associations with politicians on the left. On December 29, late at night, Shidzue was released and returned home.

Confronting the Future

On December 17, while the baroness was being interrogated at the local jail, five police detectives conducted a thorough search of her clinic. The young doctor who was present told Shidzue later that the raiders had taken away patient records, receipts, cash books, hundreds of letters from women, and her mail register book, which listed mailings of contraceptives; in sum, all of the records essential to the work of the clinic and incriminating to her. On January 31, Shidzue was summoned to the Metropolitan Police Board in Tokyo, where she was told by the police to close her clinic. They explained that whereas the large population had seemed a serious problem in the past, it was now believed that population growth was necessary for national expansion and development. Therefore, the work of her clinic contradicted official policy. She received a warning from the **Imperial Household Agency** as well. Her lawyer persuaded her that she could not fight the power of Japan's autocratic authorities and so, on February 8, she closed her clinic.

In response to a newspaper article announcing the closing, a rush of people called or dropped by to ask frantically where they would be able to obtain contraceptives in the future. Shidzue continued to receive a stream of letters from rural women as well, who had not heard of the closing. She answered these letters and sent what supplies she had available from her own home under her personal name. This courageous act was in direct contradiction of the demands and orders of the Metropolitan Police Board, the Imperial Household Agency, and members of her family.

As the war in China continued, Shidzue found it more difficult to obtain necessary birth-control supplies than to circumvent police on the lookout for thought criminals. Rubber and metal, needed to make contraceptives, were scarce and their distribution was closely monitored by the government. Given the opposition to birth-control education, there was no legal supply for Shidzue to tap; she had to rely on the small amounts of materials sent from America. The fact that she received supplies from abroad and that, from her home, she continued to provide literature and contraceptives bore witness to the low profile which a female social activist could maintain even in a repressive political environment.

By July 1938, Shidzue had only four to six months worth of supplies left. About one hundred old and new clients continued to contact her each month. How could she smuggle contraceptive materials past the officials? One ingenious, if risky, route was to have people in Sanger's organization send supplies to her brother, Hirota Yôji, who was serving at that time as a member of the Consul General's staff in San Francisco. He would then distribute this contraband to other officials who were willing to transport it home in diplomatic luggage. Unfortunately, Hirota was promoted and returned to Tokyo at the end of 1938, closing this mail service.

More frequently, Shidzue asked her American friends to send literature and contraceptives directly to her home address. These would automatically end up at the customs house in Yokohama, where she would be required to collect them in person. Had the boxes' contents, deliberately mislabeled, been checked, the smallest penalty would have been confiscation of the goods. Happily, none of them was ever opened.

Certainly her public activities had to be curtailed, and, eventually, halted altogether. Just the same, as a woman and therefore a person whose political past could soon be forgotten, she continued, for two more years, to advocate birth control and to supply necessary contraceptives and literature. Though Shidzue did this from the privacy of her home, it was still an expression of great courage in an environment of official harassment. In her quiet way, she had maintained a window of freedom during an authoritarian crackdown.

Shidzue was forced to spend only two weeks in jail; however, many of her friends and associates were less fortunate. As Ishimoto wrote to America, "[the arrested are] well known and distinguished people in our intellectual society. . . Thus the fascistic storm is sweeping the way, and we are really frightened [about] what will happen next. Like Germany, our jails have been crowded with liberals. So many friends of mine are being shut behind bars. Japan is laboring to give birth to a New Japan and under this process so many fine people are forced to sacrifice their lives."

Shidzue could make comparisons with Germany and write about militarist terrors to her American friends because, unlike most of her compatriots, she had regular access to *The New York Times* and *The Christian Science Monitor* through friendships with their respective foreign correspondents. She also received clippings and news from missionary friends. Consequently, her knowledge of the war was far broader than most of her neighbors. Unlike most of her compatriots she knew the war was not merely a chastisement but a bloodbath. At dinners and lunches, which she was privileged to enjoy with Western diplomats, missionaries, correspondents, and businessmen and/or their wives, she had direct access to uncensored news. She treasured this window of truth even though it was terrifying in its tragic detail. On August 6, 1939, she wrote in her diary, "Until this is over, I will live in this insane Japan and mix with these insane Japanese, while I await the return of law and order."

Surviving the Tragedies of War

From the beginning of 1938 until the end of the war, Shidzue lived first for her beloved Kanjû's release from jail and then for the war to end. She called these years her "winter period" and, although in the beginning she continued her political crusades sometimes openly but primarily covertly, she saw the entire period as one of marking time, sadness, and grief. Though she lamented in a letter to America, "Birth control is a forgotten word here," she added that quiet activities were not interfered with. She kept mentally alert and intellectually stimulated by reading, writing, and by discussion, especially with foreign friends. Her research and translation projects produced first the history of Japanese women for Beard's international encyclopedia; then a translation of the war novel *Wheat and Soldiers* for publication in America; and finally, drafts of articles for an American journalist friend. Until the last allied journalist, diplomat, or missionary was jailed or repatriated in 1942, she sought friendship, uncensored news, and international camaraderie among Japan's foreign community. In quiet moments at home she read a variety of Western and Japanese thinkers, novelists, and poets. She particularly found solace in the heavy, dreary Russian novels by Tolstoy and Dostoevsky. Personally, she managed with help from her estranged husband and her family to support herself and her college student sons, in spite of the ever-increasing hardships brought about by Japan's wartime economy.

Women and the Militarist Cause

Shidzue was not the only liberal woman choked by the militarist atmosphere. In fact, by the late thirties, few liberal women actively promoted progressive causes. For example, the most well-known socialist, Yamakawa Kikue, had retired to a farm outside Tokyo and was quietly raising ducks. Others struggled on, but had to compromise their principles more and more. One last political push occurred in December 1938. At that time Shidzue joined a group of women representing the Women's Suffrage League as they made one last attempt to address the issue of women's participation in politics. They failed. Soon all women's organizations were either forced to dissolve or to fall in line with government views through reorganization into approved groups. Most women joined the large government-sponsored organizations. Shidzue's liberal friends tended to join a small umbrella group, the Japan League of Women's Organizations. These women tried to advance issues such as child care, health care, livelihood, sanitation, working conditions, and social services by working with the government.

The two official government organizations, the **Greater Japan Defense Women's Association** and the **Patriotic Women's Association,** grew in the late thirties to memberships of about eight million and three million respectively. The army dominated the first one under the patronage of the Ministry of Defense, and ran it at the local level through groups sponsored by local army administrative units. The grassroots-based power structure of this organization, which was primarily composed of the wives of soldiers, laborers, farmers, and lower-level merchants, made it more powerful than its middle- and upper-class competitor, the Patriotic Women's Association, sponsored by the Home Ministry. Women in the national organizations wore either a white or khaki apron to show their patriotic endorsement of government policies. Members supported the war effort by lecturing, leading patriotic ceremonies, organizing funerals for the war dead, helping the families of active duty military and, in sum, waving the banner for national goals on the home front. These organizations were not concerned with women's freedom or equality. Their male leadership ensured that all governing principles were fully compatible with the traditional feudal structure of the family system and absolute loyalty to the sacred head of state, Emperor Hirohito. Women were to aid the militarist cause as mothers of soldiers, wives, factory workers, and farmers.

From Shidzue's perspective neither of the two ultra-patriotic organizations, nor any of the groups her friends had chosen, reflected her values or concerns, and so she withdrew from public organizations entirely. She was content to read and write at home. But even home was not a total haven. She was saddened by continual battles with her youngest brother, Hirô, who championed the opinions of the fascist bureaucracy, and hurt by the continued disapproval of her mother.

Mobilization and Rationing

Since the future was unreadable, under the leadership of Prime Minister Konoe bureaucratic officials and cabinet ministers, mostly military top brass, felt it necessary to enact a general mobilization policy which would ensure that public sacrifices could be easily and quickly commanded. In spite of heated opposition expressed in debates by Diet representatives, the National General Mobilization Bill was passed in March 1938. This law was necessarily broad. With a simple directive the government could institute price controls, regulate all commerce, declare items to be rationed, regulate wages, dismiss or hire workers, outlaw strikes, regulate financial institutions, place vital industries under government control, censor the press and radio, levy wartime taxes, require and regulate savings, and more, all without recourse to further legislation.

The rationing and induced shortages represented a psychological preparation of the people for future all-out mobilization, rather than providing essential material for the current war. It was not until July 1940, when Prime Minister Konoe formed his second cabinet, that the Mobilization Law of 1938 began to cause real hardships. At that time Konoe's new Minister of War, Tôjô Hideki, insisted on the development of an overall mobilization plan complete with tightened government economic and social controls.

Conditions before 1940 only hinted at hardships to come. Just the same, Shidzue complained about shortages that decreased her family's already modest standard of living. "Arata and Tamio must go to school with 'geta' when the three pairs of shoes they now possess are worn out. This month the amount of gasoline for a private car was cut to 1.3 gallons a day," Shidzue wrote. In a diary entry for August 1 she wrote that her maid complained that each time she went out to buy bread the yen had been reduced in value, and, to add further insult, she was confronted by rude soldiers in the local store. Commenting on gasoline rationing, Shidzue objected heatedly to the scoffers and cheaters who selfishly used illegal means to ensure their own full tanks. At this point, however, the family was not really suffering. After all, they still had shoes to wear out, cash to purchase available goods, and they owned a car, which made gasoline rationing of interest. Just the same, the war with China was beginning to take an economic toll, especially in rising inflation and selective shortages of goods needed by the military.

A Proud Mother

In March 1939, Shidzue rejoiced in her sons' educational achievements. Arata graduated in biology from Tokyo's aristocratic Peers' School. Under the exclusive control of the Imperial Household, this was the school of choice for the imperial family, members of the old nobility, and selected others who were educated there by the will of His Imperial Majesty. In April, one month following his graduation, Arata enrolled in the science division at Kyoto Imperial University. He would be twenty-two the following June.

Tamio also graduated from higher school in March 1939; he would be twenty-one in October. He had concentrated on literature at Daiichi, First Higher School of Tokyo. Following the pattern set forward in the University Ordinance of 1918, by the time he entered this higher school he had completed eight years of elementary training and four years of middle school. This prestigious public school, the oldest higher school in Japan, was founded in 1875. Two years later it was named preparatory higher school for Tokyo Imperial University and placed under the university's direction. Completion of the three-year preparatory course almost guaranteed placement at that premier national university. On March 21, when the list of successful entrants was posted, Tamio's name was among them.

When Tamio entered the Daiichi Higher School he was bewitched by the atmosphere and begged his mother to permit him to live in the dormitory. In his final year before college she acquiesced. A characteristic feature of higher-school dormitories throughout Japan was the emphasis on student self-government. Naturally, Tamio was elated when he was chosen chairman of his dormitory.

Enthusiastically he devoted most of his energy to this respected role.

The elected office of dormitory chairman represented the pinnacle within the public school hierarchy of the Education Ministry's enforced self-government activities. Beginning in elementary school these exercises were designed to produce students who exhibited the desired qualities of self-discipline and social cooperation, and would become adults who served society with appropriate civic attitudes and beliefs. The dormitory chairman was expected to work with and oversee all committees, which were in charge of meals, books, student activities, the school newspaper, and auditing all of the expenses for these services. Tamio, therefore, chaired all business that was transacted for the more than two hundred and fifty students in the dormitory, coordinated elected committees, and met, as well, with the chairmen and committee heads of the other dormitories.

Tamio's election as chairman was exhilarating, but the work was exhausting and by the time he graduated he was physically run down. Unfortunately this last year at Daiichi coincided with a health crisis, a steady increase in the numbers of tuberculosis victims. Although in principle TB victims were mostly the elderly and people living in unsanitary conditions, young students were also exposed to this disease in heavily increasing numbers. Dormitory life with its crowded conditions was acknowledged as a breeding ground for the disease. In the winter of 1939, just before he was to enter Tokyo Imperial University, Tamio was diagnosed with tuberculosis.

Elation, Despair, and Tragedy

Ever since her beloved Kanjû's imprisonment, Shidzue thought of him many times each day. She remained close to him through her private diary, and through letters and news transmitted between them by his lawyer. On November 28, 1939, Kanjû had been permitted to leave his cell briefly to visit his wife, who was in the hospital undergoing an operation for uterine cancer. Kanjû's lawyer, who was charged with taking the prisoner from his cell to the hospital, arranged a meeting at his office between his client and Shidzue. Though the meeting was only one hour, her joy knew no bounds. One month later, on December 28, Tamio burst into the house shouting, "Mother, Mr. Katô has returned." He had read this report in the morning *Nichi Nichi Newspaper*. Shidzue was ecstatic. This joy was soon eclipsed.

In early 1940, Tamio's health began to visibly deteriorate. From that time on Tamio was confined to home. Due to shortages and rationing, Shidzue found it difficult to provide adequate nutrition and medicine for her son. Most probably in 1942 recovery would have been impossible under the best dietary and medical conditions. In those days, even in America, diagnosis of TB was received as a death sentence.

Arata returned home in September 1942. Shidzue, consumed with anxiety and exhausted over Tamio's care, was overjoyed to see him, even though she knew that soon he would have to leave for military service. Since he had a college degree, however, she believed that he would qualify for the officers' training corps. A career as an army officer would have been fitting considering the distinguished military career of his grandfather Ishimoto and the fact that two of his father's brothers currently served as army generals. But first he must wait for the draft notice. He did not wait long. About ten days after his return in September he received the dreaded "red letter." The military affairs clerks throughout Japan, who kept records of every eligible draftee, were very efficient and their counterparts in the military draft offices delivered the list of notifications without a break. On October 1,

Private Ishimoto Arata reported for duty, assigned to the transportation corps as a truck driver. Shidzue despaired over the loss of her recently returned son, and once again was alone with the gravely ill Tamio.

Pearl Harbor

Shidzue had received her last letter from Mary Beard shortly before the December 7 bombing of Pearl Harbor. In it Beard wrote that even if the relationship between Japan and the United States worsens, "Our friendship will not change." Reflecting on this moment Shidzue said that when the reality of war took hold, Beard's words became even more important to her. She hoped that all her American friendships would withstand this ultimate horror.

Japan and the United States had been conducting negotiations toward averting war for some time, but by the early fall of 1941 Japanese cabinet ministers at Imperial Headquarters, most particularly the military leadership, had determined that Japan's survival in the Far East required military action. They believed that Western actions of the past several decades had been designed to destroy the Japanese empire.

Japan's case for war was founded on Western attitudes of superiority that manifested themselves in treaties and agreements in which Japan was forced into a subservient position. Even the pro-American Tsurumi Yûsuke on his American lecture tour in 1926 had quietly noted that his countrymen had been distressed by anti-Japanese actions and immigration laws that treated Japanese as inferiors. He complained most particularly about the 1924 immigration law, which excluded all Japanese. Then there were the naval reduction conferences of the twenties and early thirties at which the Japanese always came up short. When Japan set up colonies in imitation of Western imperialism, the West objected. After Manchuria was brought into Japan's sphere of influence, the League of Nations voted to condemn Japan, a League member. In the 1930s Japanese officials cited one attempt after another by the Western powers to limit Japan's empire and to destroy its economic livelihood. The situation worsened with the China war, and the escalating of an embargo system by President Franklin Roosevelt, designed to cut Japan off from needed supplies such as oil, steel, and airplanes. By 1941, when the U.S. government imposed a total embargo on all petroleum products, Japanese leaders concluded their country was about to be destroyed. They saw themselves surrounded by the ABCD powers (American, British, Chinese, and Dutch) who were determined to bring them first to submission and then to annihilation.

On December 1, 1941, the Imperial Conference agreed to Admiral Yamamoto Isoroku's plan for a preemptive strike against the United States at Pearl Harbor. Yamamoto, a brilliant naval officer, had studied in America and had great admiration for her military strength. Although he initiated the plan to wipe out the U.S. Navy stationed in Hawaii, he believed there was only a small chance of success. He reasoned that if Japan struck hard enough the United States would be too crippled to retaliate and a treaty neutralizing the Americans could be negotiated. Others in the conference were more positive, and even believed that Japan could win a war with the United States. Everyone, including the emperor, supported this strike against the U.S. Navy as necessary if Japan was to defend its integrity against the encircling Western powers.

Family Tragedy

After the outbreak of war with the United States, Shidzue found it more and more difficult to leave the house to search for black-market food and medicine for her desperately ill son. Besides, Tamio did not like to be left alone, for at any moment some member of the **neighborhood association** (*tonarigumi*) might call out from the front entryway and disturb his rest.

Order Number Seventeen, titled Essentials of Providing for Community Councils, had been issued by the Home Ministry on September 11, 1940. This directive formed the basis of the wartime neighborhood association, which required that about ten households within a given area be organized into a unit run by a council, which would then direct each neighbor's participation in the moral training, spiritual unity, and economic stability of the community. The activities of each neighborhood association were extensive and participation mandatory. Essentially, it was up to the council and its chairman to administer the rationing system. They would have to determine distribution of scarce goods according to size and needs of families under their jurisdiction. As early as the winter of 1940–1941, *tonarigumi* were responsible for distributing charcoal for the cold months ahead and making sure that the neighborhood and then each family receive an appropriate share of staples such as rice, sugar, and matchsticks, which by June 1940 had been rationed. Small-shop owners were also assisted by the neighborhood association in their acquisition of tools and stock, and fair distribution was monitored on a daily and monthly basis. Every day someone delivered a circular to each household, which might contain vital information about foodstuffs, but would also announce deaths in the neighborhood, deaths of neighbors' sons fighting abroad, and names of sons returning from a tour of duty or about to leave. In this way neighbors learned about available rations and were alerted to their obligation to show solidarity with others by offering sympathy and assistance to a bereaved family or, armed with blazing sun flags, by joyously sending a new recruit off to the front.

By April 1941, a ration book system was in place and the list of rationed items increased. After war with the United States began, it was obvious to everyone that the allotment of rice per person per day was lower than that required by a healthy adult. Shortages had become severe. By February, *misô,* soy sauce, potatoes, bread, cooking oil, and vegetables, among other food items, were added to the list of rationed foods, and the protein-rich produce, fish, eggs, and tofu—as well as the grains housewives used to augment the reduced rice servings—required ration coupons. Clothing was also placed on a rationing system, with each person receiving a coupon book of one hundred points to be used for everything bought during the year: socks (two points), coats (fifty points), blouses (eight points), and so forth. Everything manufactured, from dry goods to finished products, had a point equivalent and was supposed to be carefully monitored. In response to the impoverished legal market in all foodstuffs and commodities, black markets sprang up simultaneously with each new regulation. At the same time, all food and material necessary for the military effort were diverted from the civilian population. It was the responsibility of the neighborhood association to administer the rationing system and to make sure that the rules of distribution and usage were fairly administered. Sometimes this was efficiently accomplished and sometimes chairmen and councils took advantage of their positions of power for their own gain, or favored neighbors and relatives.

Shidzue remembered her neighborhood association as thoughtful and kind, and said that they recognized the special burden of her family circumstances. They compassionately shortened, as far as possible, her participation in required air raid exercises and her contribution to the community's labor services. They did not refrain, however, from bringing around announcements or making deliveries when she was out trying to procure, often through the black market, additional protein-rich food or medicine for Tamio. While she was gone, a member of the neighborhood association might bring around a circular. The neighbor would open the sliding front door and call out in a loud voice from the entryway, expecting someone inside to come read and stamp the letter.

Just before Arata left for the war zone on April 22, 1943, he telephoned his mother, at which time she told her elder son that in the months to come his first duty was to survive. Furthermore, she told him that he should permit himself to be taken prisoner, if possible, and use his ability to speak English to his advantage. This, of course, was directly contrary to army orders, which demanded that as a loyal subject of his imperial majesty, he should fight to the death, and never surrender to the enemy.

On June 26, Arata's twenty-sixth birthday, his brother Tamio died. In a letter to Arata about his brother's death Shidzue wrote, "With his father holding his left hand and his mother holding his right hand, our beloved Tamio, quietly and peacefully, slipped into an everlasting sleep." On July 3 Shidzue wrote to Kanjû informing him of the sad event. She then told him of her own terrible ordeal. She had not stepped foot outside her door from April 19 until the day of the funeral, and had not been able to meet with anyone, speak to anyone, or write letters. The awesome responsibility of caring for Tamio had forced her to live a life she would not have chosen, "the life of a Catholic nun." Now she was drawing a line, cutting off her past from her future. What did he think of this new plan? She asked him to call at the earliest opportunity.

Shidzue was completely alone; both sons were gone, one to the war and the other to the grave. Ishimoto Keikichi, the shame of the family, remained her husband but they were bound only by the family register. She thought of herself as a widow. Just before New Year's Day 1944, she moved to a smaller house. From that moment she felt free to think of her own life as a woman. Shidzue reflected, "Though I had passed the period of a young woman's passions, I had feelings which must find a home." It was from this time that Kanjû began to visit regularly once again.

Personal Joy Amidst Bombs of Destruction

By 1944, Shidzue felt free to marry. There were still obstacles, for she must once again contend with the feudal family system. Kanjû, on the other hand, was now a widower since his wife had died of cancer in 1941. As a released political prisoner, he continued to be watched by the special higher police, and could not participate in any political or labor organization. He made a slim living as a newspaper columnist for the *Tokyo Mainichi Newspaper.* At this time his teenage daughter and son lived with relatives.

Shidzue recounted Kanjû's proposal. "After a while he asked me to marry him. It was a totally awkward proposal. His manner of proposing was to say, 'My comrades are searching for a second wife for me and I cannot fight against them. If you can't marry me I will have to marry someone else.'" Shidzue accepted and began the process of securing papers of permission from the Imperial Household Agency to show to officials at the civil office who could then grant the divorce. This time she was able to enlist the support of two male members of her family so that the Imperial Household Agency would consider the matter. Her elder brother, Hirota Kôichi, and her brother-in-law, Ichikawa Yoshitaro, at that time a member of the Foreign Affairs Ministry, offered her petition. They justified their action to family members saying that since she no longer had sons at home, her responsibilities to the Ishimoto family had been fulfilled.

The divorce was granted in November 1944 and her name was stricken from the Ishimoto family register. Shidzue, now forty-seven, and Kanjû, fifty-two, planned to be married immediately in spite of continued opposition from some of her family. Her mother and her mother's brother, Tsurumi Sadao, in particular, continued to grumble. They felt it was degrading for someone of Shidzue's status to marry a labor organizer with a proletarian class background. Uncle Sadao, an officer in the army, found it especially embarrassing that he would have to acknowledge a member of the family who had ties to the left wing. The wedding was not to be stopped, but the ceremony would take place in Kyoto away from the site of family conflict, and away from the first severe American bombing raids over Tokyo.

On their return to Tokyo, Kanjû and Shidzue rented a newly built house that had been abandoned by its owner who sought peace in the countryside. At the time of the move they discussed what to do about Shidzue's extensive trousseau of clothing and furnishings she had brought to her first marriage. Kanjû told her that all she need bring this time was herself; and so it was decided that her accumulated property of thirty years would be left behind, and she moved only a few things in a small cart. Kanjû's two children joined their father and stepmother. The following winter, March 30, 1945, the family grew to five with the birth of a new baby, Shidzue's miracle child, Takiko, "great joy."

Shidzue wrote jubilantly about this miracle. "The impossible became possible. Yes, something that one as worldly as myself would call unimaginable actually happened. The child I had long desired was born. . . . I was quite old to become pregnant. Twenty eight years had passed since my last pregnancy. I had to seize this last chance. . . . I believed that the new life sleeping in my womb was given me in exchange for the life of my lost son."

She was not at all concerned that the child would be born just four months after her official marriage to Kanjû. Writing publicly about this for the first time in her ninetieth year, she dispensed with the issue in a few sentences. After describing details of her marriage, she continued, "A short time afterwards I was blessed with a daughter, Takiko. I was 48 years old. She was born on March 30, 1945. Since my marriage ceremony was performed in November of the previous year, there were people who made much of the trivial fact that the months did not add up. But from our perspective our real marriage had taken place when we began living together in March 1944."

Shortly before she was to give birth, the most severe bombing raid of the war occurred over Tokyo. This single raid of March 9–10 is said to have killed over two hundred thousand people. General Curtis B. LeMay, who directed the firebombing, called it a "diller." Radio Tokyo called it "slaughter bombing" telling of the "sea of flame which enclosed the residential and commercial sections of Tokyo." During the rest of March, throughout April and on into May, General LeMay followed up with intensive bombing, delivered by low-flying B-29s, over Tokyo and throughout Japan.

In spite of this public terror, Shidzue's private miracle continued. Unlike every other night, March 30, the night of Takiko's birth, was calm. "There were no shrill, ear piercing sounds of the sirens, no electric failures, and no water stoppages. My midwife said this was a blessing given by the gods," Shidzue remembered. She delivered her baby that night at home. Four nights later the skies were once again filled with death, but while others ran out to find shelter, Shidzue stayed home, and covered her new baby with a blanket to shut out the sounds of the planes, explosions, and wailing sirens. The baby slept, and the house remained intact. "It's a miracle," she cried out.

On the evening of May 23, the bombing finally came to the Katôs' section of Tokyo. Putting the baby in a basket, they left the house. First they went to the shelter Kanjû had dug, carrying with them just two bottles of milk for Takiko. The bombs fell nearby and the fires were less than a mile away. A house just a few yards away burned down. With the help of a young couple they managed to extinguish the flames that threatened their own home. Finally, beneath a sky ablaze with lights of "B-san," they had to flee. Not knowing where to go they simply wandered about searching for water, keeping to the narrow streets. Worn out, they sheltered under a bridge, about two train stops from their home, and prayed. For the next twenty to thirty minutes they watched what seemed like a typhoon of fire. Tired, discouraged, and without direction, they decided to return home. The first sight they saw was the burned-out rubble of their neighbor's house. The houses all around theirs were razed to the ground. Their house remained untouched. As Shidzue entered her home, she called out "Kamisama (god), thank you."

Over the next few months they survived. Kanjû suffered from acute inflammation of the kidney, a condition brought on by fatigue and lack of adequate nourishment. Hearing of his illness, friends from his old labor union and associates among the intelligentsia brought the family food. They brought pumpkins, the new staple, and, most important, milk for Takiko that they purchased on the black market. With this help, miraculous luck, their own determination, and Shidzue's trips to the countryside to find food, the family all survived to experience the surrender and the occupation of their homeland by the enemy.

VI

Campaigning for a Democratic Society

The **Allied Occupation** officially began with the signing of the documents of surrender on the battleship *Missouri* on September 2, 1945. A short time later the Katôs were visited by an American serviceman newly stationed in Japan. Shidzue had just returned from her regular trip to the countryside in search of food. It had been a "difficult journey on trains crowded beyond imagination—a journey in which I carried on my back a large rucksack filled with potatoes, so heavy that I fell many times as I walked along the bomb-torn street from the station to my house." She was astonished to see an American jeep parked there. Lt. Tom Tsukahara had come "to confirm that we had no trace of war crimes in our background." Later in September both Katôs were invited to GHQ to discuss labor and women's issues.

In fact the U.S. government had previously cleared both Katôs of militarist sympathies. From 1941 to 1944 the intelligence department in Washington, known then as the Office of Strategic Services, had collected information on Japanese nationals. One such file, labeled Friendly Persons and containing just a few cards, included a report headed

"Baroness Shidzue (Hirota) Ishimoto," dating from 1941. In it a former missionary to Japan testified that "Baroness Ishimoto is reported as being anti-militaristic, and pro American."

Information on Kanjû came primarily from a June 22, 1945, report that the Director of Security and Intelligence in Washington had obtained in an interview with Darley Downs, a Congregational missionary, who had lived and taught in Japan from 1919–1941. He described thirty-nine Japanese whom he believed would be helpful to the American authorities. Both Katô Kanjû and Shidzue's Uncle, Tsurumi Yûsuke, were on the list.

It is not surprising, then, that Mr. and Mrs. Katô were taken to the offices of the **Civil Information and Education Section (CIE)** at the **General Headquarters (GHQ)** of the **Supreme Commander of the Allied Powers (SCAP)** for discussion during that first chaotic month of the **American Occupation.** Shidzue's interviewers asked her what Japanese women would most want to achieve in the postwar era. She replied that they would want to secure their fundamental rights as human beings. When asked to be more specific, she educated her questioners with a brief history of prewar women's movements that had purposefully sought to secure political and social liberation for women. The interviewers expressed astonishment that Japanese women understood democratic principles and had already demanded political rights. In conclusion, Shidzue stressed that the creation of a democratic Japan without full participation of women would be meaningless.

Political Activism

August 1945 had been one of the most devastating and destructive months of the war for Japanese in the home islands. Bad news followed bad news in quick succession. On August 6th the first nuclear bomb was dropped, killing and injuring over a hundred thousand people in Hiroshima. On August 8, the Soviets informed the Japanese government that as of the next day a state of war would exist between them. On August 9, the second nuclear bomb was dropped on Nagasaki, with predictably terrible results. To top it off General LeMay once again sent fire bombers in to select cities on August 14. Finally, Emperor Hirohito put his power behind the government faction that voted to accept the Potsdam Declaration and on August 15, Japan formally surrendered unconditionally. The people were stunned, exhausted, and, in many cases, relieved.

The emperor's broadcast announcing the end of the war motivated activist men and women to begin life again amid the ruins of war. Within ten days of surrender Katô Kanjû had arranged a Tokyo meeting for past leaders of socialist parties. As before the war, women were excluded from this gathering and seemingly from future participation. Even the left remained unanimously imbued with its prewar sense of inequality.

Women, however, did not wait for invitations from men to begin their political activity. On August 25, seventy-two women joined to form the Women's Committee on Postwar Countermeasures. These women had been prominent in a variety of prewar and wartime activities extending from early protests against the militarists to full support for the war effort. Although they represented a broad spectrum of viewpoints, all were agreed on their determination to fight for equality with men and full political rights.

It took Katô Shidzue a few weeks longer to find her role in the new Japan. But then, she had a six-month-old baby to care for and a husband too busy with national politics to help out at home. Like other Tokyoites, Shidzue found sustaining life amid the rubble of destruction in the fall of

1945 a full-time job. Although the Katôs were more fortunate than most, for their house had withstood the bombing, Shidzue still had to make arduous trips to the countryside in search of food. New political activities would not provide nourishment for her daughter. Even so, contact with SCAP officials and observation of her husband's political activities generated an excitement that she found impossible to resist.

Lt. Ethel B. Weed joined the staff at CIE in October. Her job as Women's Information Officer in the Women's Affairs Branch was to formulate policy in areas affecting Japanese women and to develop programs that would provide information relevant to their integration into all aspects of the new society, including their political, economic, and social democratization. Lt. Weed immediately began assembling Japanese women who had been active in suffrage and social movements before the war. Katô Shidzue, a prominent member of this group, had ready access to Weed's office from this moment on.

Campaigning for the Diet

By November 1945, Shidzue had decided that her contribution to the new democratic Japan would be elective politics. She had not yet determined a party affiliation; in fact, no women had been invited to join any postwar party, and it was not yet legal for women to vote or run for office. It was Shidzue's trust in the American promise of equal political rights for women that gave her the vision to project a professional future not yet possible.

On October 10, General Douglas MacArthur ordered the new prime minister, Shidehara Kijûrô, to force Diet enactment of five basic principles, the first of which demanded passage of an election law providing women the right to vote and run for office. The Diet which was to legislate this change consisted of sitting wartime members primarily from established parties on the right. After much debate and foot dragging, this wartime Diet passed MacArthur's demanded equal rights elective law on December 15. A month before this legislative action, on November 14, Katô Shidzue became the first woman to announce her candidacy for a seat in the House of Representatives at such time as new election laws permitted.

Everyone expected January elections. SCAP, however, first wanted to purge public officials considered responsible for the war. The **purge** directive effectively removed at least eighty-three percent of the incumbent representatives. Hardest hit were the members of what had become the Progressive Party, which lost 260 of its 274 founding members, including Secretary-General Tsurumi Yûsuke, Shidzue's favorite uncle. Even the new socialist party was decimated. Of the original seventeen founders ten were purged, representing ten of twelve sitting Diet members. Elections were set for April 10, and the newly reconstituted parties scrambled for candidates. Kanjû announced for the **Japan Socialist Party (JSP).** Shidzue, who began her campaign as an independent, also joined the JSP ranks later.

Newspapers highlighted Shidzue as the first woman to seek government office. She was identified as the former Baroness Ishimoto, founder of Japan's prewar birth-control movement and an associate of the famous American birth-control advocate Margaret Sanger. In interviews she always spoke first about her 1937 arrest, establishing her anti-militarist credentials. Then she stressed her campaign issues: democratization of women's lives and promotion of family planning. For her, control of family size was inextricably intertwined with improved quality of life, and both were essential if women were to enjoy equality with men.

Shidzue's campaign was a frugal undertaking. She walked all over Tokyo's large second district, megaphone in hand, seeking votes. Whenever she could, she gave lectures, spoke at schools, put up posters, and gave speeches on street corners. It was a populist campaign. Admitting that her political statements were not theoretical or philosophical, but, rather, practical, she would tell her constituents, "If I am elected I will ask for increases in rations of rice, sugar and tobacco." She recognized that Japan, a defeated nation, had to ask its conquerors for everything and so she urged the people to go to GHQ and ask for staples, for meat, and to ask that Japanese soldiers be returned home immediately.

From the beginning Shidzue recognized the usefulness of radio for educating her constituents. Fortunately, her associations with CIE afforded her substantial radio access both on the air and behind the scenes, and she became adroit at building support through frequent use of air time. She would hitchhike rides in GI jeeps, saying, "I am electioneering and I need to get from here to the radio station to make a political announcement. Could you take me?" This campaign method reached more people in less time than leg power and megaphones. Radio was critical to Shidzue's success.

Radio was crucial to SCAP's plans to democratize the country also. One of its first actions had been to take advisory control of radio broadcasting, and U.S. officials continued to direct and censor this medium throughout the occupation period (1945–1952). Radio programming was expected to advance concepts of peace and security, aid the establishment of a democratic government, and protect the rights and freedoms of the people as defined by Occupation directives.

Shidzue agreed with SCAP's evaluation of radio's potential for generating political and social change, and so she accepted an invitation to join the Japanese committee created by SCAP to advise the **Broadcasting Corporation of Japan (BCJ, later NHK)**. In this way she gained access to radio broadcasting for her own political campaign, could help Lt. Weed's Women's Affairs Branch launch various educational programs for women, and had a new medium through which to propagate family planning.

One of the most successful daytime programs inaugurated was the "Women's Hour." This was a daily show that encouraged women to exchange ideas on social and political issues and highlighted women's new political rights and the April elections. Evening programming was especially useful for political candidates, and Shidzue gained further exposure through regular participation. For example, in December she was a guest on "Round Table of the Air." The featured topic that evening was "Women's Place in Japanese Democracy," a controversial issue in spite of the new voting rights law. During the discussion Katô and the home minister, the first highly placed government official to appear on such a program, squared off on the general question of women's participation in politics versus women's performance of traditional roles in the home. This was probably the first serious public debate of public versus private roles for women. The nature of the discussion called into question substantial sections of Japan's family system as embodied in the Meiji Civil Code of 1898. The home minister was a perfect foil for Katô, "who displayed a feminist attitude" as she took the radical side in defense of womanhood. This was her first opportunity to speak against the traditional family system and the way in which it imprisoned and oppressed women, a theme she would continue to emphasize in the Diet after her election.

Democracy Defined

Katô Shidzue believed that a democratic revolution would bring about the "new Japan." On this point she was in agreement with Kanjû, their associates in the Socialist Party and their political competitors to the left, the **Japan**

Communist Party (JCP); however, the definition of these two words "democratic revolution" was different for all who embraced them. For Shidzue they meant realization of an American-style democracy imbued with equality for men and women brought about through peaceful elections. She believed that Occupation officials would support people like herself in their quest for adequate economic welfare for women and children, protection of families in which husband and wife were equal, and individual social and political freedom. When she spoke more concretely she specified a national health program, particularly protective of women and children, a basic level of livelihood protection, nationalization of the communications and transportation systems and of primary heavy industry. These specific programs were reflective of her socialist perspective, learned during the thirties from Kanjû, and were in no way related to American democratic theory or practice.

In fact her vision for society was more closely akin to Britain's postwar Labor Party program than anything she had seen in America. It was, however, an idealized image of American democracy that packaged her vision. She opposed the ideology of the Communist Party and any abandonment of economic capitalism. She assumed that the Socialists would grow in strength, and, with the help of newly liberated women, would bring this democratic revolution about peacefully, without Communist Party assistance. The reactionary and conservative right would pose no problem, she believed, thanks to SCAP's purge of prewar militarist sympathizers. In her first few months of working with CIE and SCAP's government section, she had become convinced that the Americans would help create the revolution that would bring about this new Japan. She did not dwell on any contradiction between the socialist component of her vision and the more moderate American perspective, which emphasized individual accomplishment over nationalization of social programs and industry.

All signs seemed to support Shidzue's perspective. The Socialists, in spite of their divisions, had formulated a platform that would improve the lives of all members of their natural constituency from farmers to workers, from returned servicemen to women and families, indeed the great majority of the population. Officials at SCAP appeared to be backing the Socialists. The communist opposition was small, and a purge of the conservatives promised to decimate their strength. Economically, Japan in 1945 and early 1946 was worse-off than it had been in the last year of the war. Something had to be done if the people were merely to survive, let alone rise from the ashes. Some form of social democracy seemed to be the answer. Given SCAP's interest in constitutional reform—which would assure universal suffrage for all adults, freedom to organize for labor, land reform for farmers, and basic economic livelihood for everyone—a democratic revolution seemed assured. Since Shidzue forced her idealization of democracy, or more accurately, democratic socialism, to fit with her experiences in America, it is not surprising that she believed the Americans at SCAP were like-minded and would help create a new Japan conforming to her principles. She would soon discover that neither SCAP's goals nor those of her country's leaders agreed with her conceptualization of a democratic society. She would further discover that automatic support from the Americans for socialist causes should not be assumed and that she and the Socialist Party should not have counted out the old right guard so soon.

A Women's Club for Democratic Activism

During the first months of 1946, however, Shidzue was euphoric. She sensed a meeting of minds with her CIE mentor, Ethel Weed, and with her prewar associates on the question of democracy. Weed saw her mandate to be to encourage organizations that would be both activist and educational and would spread throughout the nation growing in membership, numbers, and sophistication. She began sharing this vision with individual women who came to her office and credited Katô with organizing the Women's Democratic Club, "the first really new organization to come out of the occupation. . . ."

The core of the Women's Democratic Club consisted of Katô Shidzue, Matsuoka Yôko, and Hani Setsuko, all well known at CIE. Matsuoka often served as an interpreter, and Weed frequently called on Hani and Katô for advice and information. Five more influential women were then added to the group. Hani suggested Miyamoto Yuriko and Sata Ineko, and Katô suggested Yamamoto Sugi, Akamatsu Tsuneko, and Yamamuro Tamiko. The preparatory committee of eight drew in fifteen more women with varied backgrounds and interests.

The original eight participants were women who had known one another before the war and who were determined to work for a democratic Japan. Matsuoka Yôko, a journalist and interpreter, had lived in the United States in the thirties, graduating from Swarthmore College in 1939. Hani Setsuko, also descended from the elite Matsuoka family, was Yôko's cousin. Her mother, Hani Motoko, a Christian, was a noted prewar journalist and educator. During the thirties and early forties both mother and daughter had assisted the wartime government in a program of economic rationalization, and Setsuko had run a school in Beijing for Japanese children. After the war she advocated women's suffrage and other liberal causes.

Both Miyamoto Yuriko and Sata Ineko were writers with prewar and postwar ties to the Communist Party. Miyamoto was married to the well-known communist Miyamoto Kenji, who served twelve years in jail for his communist activities and after the war became a significant force in the Japan Communist Party (JCP). Yuriko was in and out of jail a half dozen times during the thirties and forties, suffering severe injury to her health. (She died in 1951 at the age of fifty-two.) In the forties, like so many writers, she joined a literary organization approved by the militarists. Although she claimed that she refused to renounce her political views, she did associate willingly with pro-government writers. After the war she worked with various women's organizations, and the Communist Party, and wrote her most highly praised novels. She was welcomed at CIE, as were several communists during those early months. At Katô's suggestion, Miyamoto joined her as a member of the BCJ Advisory Committee on radio broadcasting. Miyamoto represented the most left-wing perspective within the Women's Democratic Club, and she and Katô locked ideological horns early on.

Sata, a longtime close friend of Miyamoto, was also a writer and active in both communist politics and proletarian literary groups in the twenties and thirties. She capitulated to the demands of the militarist government after her arrest in the thirties and admittedly committed *tenkô,* recanting her previous anti-government thoughts and actions. She showed her loyalty to the wartime government during the early forties by joining literary groups that traveled to China, Korea, and Southeast Asia to boost troop morale. After the war she rejoined the Communist Party but, much to her amazement, was expelled in 1951. She continued her literary endeavors during the postwar era, writing about her wartime experiences including her collaboration with the fascist government.

Akamatsu Tsuneko was a founding member of the first postwar Women's Committee created in August 1945. She had a long history of labor and feminist interests, joined the JSP as soon as women were invited, and in September 1946 became the first female chief of the JSP Women's Section. She also headed the women's section of the All Japan Labor Union. In 1947 she was elected to the Diet in the first postwar **House of Councillors** election. Akamatsu and Katô served on a number of committees together in the JSP and worked together on legislation both while Katô was in the House of Representatives and after she, too, was elected to the House of Councillors in 1950. Yamamoto Sugi was a physician and had been a member of Katô's Birth Control League in the thirties. She was much admired by Katô because she was both an activist and a knowledgeable scientist. Katô believed that Yamamoto's pointed refusal to collaborate with the wartime government, illustrated by her rejection of a high position in the Imperial Rule Assistance Association, showed great courage. Yamamuro Tamiko, a Christian, was the daughter of Yamamuro Gumpei, the founder of the Salvation Army in Japan.

The first general meeting of the Women's Democratic Club was held March 16, with about a thousand people attending. Miyamoto read the organization's three founding principles: 1. We must fight for liberation from the feudal ideas and customs which women have been forced to uphold; 2. We must pull together both in the workplace and the family and develop new and independent perspectives on our way of life; 3. We must advance Japan's new democratic achievements through exhibition of women's capabilities which, heretofore, have been suppressed. She then read her proclamation in which she condemned the wartime government for mobilizing women in support of a war that created the devastating economic circumstances under which they were now forced to suffer. She further criticized the peacetime holdover government for failing to generate new women's groups dedicated to solving their postwar problems.

An enthusiastic CIE report of March 23 commented that the Women's Democratic Club was the "first large New Democratic group for women to grow out of the Occupation." CIE was not concerned about Miyamoto's communist ideas, nor aware that an ideological split existed among the original eight founders. All important was that the general meeting had been a resounding success. The next step was the establishment of local clubs. Katô traveled widely to help women in other cities and towns start their own branches. The new local clubs became centers for discussion of women's issues and sponsors of formal conferences and lectures. The ideological conflict between Katô and Miyamoto, which had the potential to split the organization, was glossed over temporarily in the excitement of the moment and the anticipation of the upcoming April election.

Political Triumph

The first postwar election took place on April 10, 1946. There were 2,624 candidates, including 97 women, vying for 466 seats in the House of Representatives. The **purge** had resulted in deep cuts in the experienced ranks of politicians and over eighty percent of all candidates were running for the first time. It had been a long campaign, and Katô Shidzue, the first announced woman to run for office, had spent five months seeking votes. She had made effective use of both traditional campaign methods and the informal channels provided by her American connections. Her platform pressed for further extension of women's rights, positive advocacy for family planning, and general improvement of women's miserable economic circumstances. An interested public, led by the media, followed her campaign and those of other candidates closely.

Speculation about the role of women in elective politics ran the gamut in newspaper editorials and celebrity quotations. Conservative writers mistrusted the women's participation while radicals generally applauded it, though writers in all camps felt that women's influence, at least at first, would be unprogressive. A typical newswriter's con-

Kâto Shidzue takes her daughter, Taki, to the polls in Japan's first democratic election to include women voters and candidates, April 1946. Kâto Shidzue was one of the 39 women to win election to the Diet. Courtesy of Katô Shidzue.

clusion read, "Although they can become good wives and virtuous mothers, they have not been educated for public or social living."

Many well-known women commented on the potential of women in politics. The newswoman Kamichika Ichiko, known in the twenties for her love affair with the anarchist Ôsugi Sakae, wrote, "Women's suffrage means progress and is a weapon of which we must make the greatest possible use." Kamichika would become a JSP Diet representative herself in the fifties. Hirabayashi Taiko, the other woman arrested with Shidzue in 1937, said "I have heard some people say that they (women) would rather choose a pound of sweet potatoes than women's suffrage, which you can neither eat nor drink." This conclusion was foolish, Hirabayashi believed, since politicized women could work to improve the food distribution system and the education system, and thereby ensure that Japan would never again cause a tragedy. On the other hand, Ichikawa Fusae, the leading spokesperson for women's suffrage, admitted that given the choice, women would choose sugar over suffrage, that is, food over political rights. But she envisioned a bright future through education and participation in the new political system. Ironically on April 10, poll watchers would not allow her to vote, claiming she had not registered. Later, purged by the Americans, she was prevented from running for elective office until her purge was canceled in 1950.

Questions about how many eligible voters would vote, whether any women would actually be elected, how the parties and the previously inexperienced candidates would fare in the election were answered on April 10. A little over seventy-two percent of the eligible electorate voted, a few percentage points higher for men than women. Out of the 466 seats up for election 381 were filled by first-time candidates and of these 39 were women. Each of the three largest parties (Liberal, Progressive, and Socialist) elected eight women; one Communist Party member was elected; and fourteen women running with smaller parties or as independents were successful. Katô Shidzue was elected from the traditionally socialist Tokyo second district. Katô Kanjû, elected from Nagoya, was one of the few Diet members with previous experience as a national legislator. The elected husband and wife were christened *oshidori giin,* a pair of lovebird representatives, a take-off on *oshidori fûfu,* happily married lovebirds. Katô Shidzue joined the first postwar Diet with energy and optimism, excited to be involved in the legislative process. She saw her election as a watershed between preparatory activities publicizing her causes and formal action that would convert her ideas into law.

Organization of the lower house in this Ninetieth Diet focused on committee assignments with appointments effectively determined by the party leadership. Each committee was composed of members from the ruling Liberal/Progressive coalition and from the largest minority party, the JSP. Since women had still not been integrated into any of the parties, they did not have a say in the selection process and were placed on committees at the whim of their party's leadership. Katô Shidzue, undoubtedly in part due to her marriage to one of the most powerful socialist leaders, was appointed to two important committees, Budget and Constitution Revision. She took these assignments seriously and determined to be heard under extremely difficult circumstances. As a woman she was not only ignored, but also physically isolated with other elected women at the back of the chambers. Also, as a member of the opposition party Shidzue could not originate legislation or speak directly in the Diet. Even within the JSP she was relegated to the subordinate Women's Affairs Division, which was headed by a man until the next fall.

Deliberating in the Diet

None of the new female representatives had power within their parties and most did not have the political education to operate effectively from the Diet floor. Katô knew that speaking her mind at committee meetings or in general Diet sessions would be difficult but she intended, somehow, to present her agenda. During that first summer, Katô earned the respect of journalists and the public as one of the few Diet women who penetrated the barriers of old political ties, ruling party power, and male domination.

On July 6, she became the first woman on the Constitution Revision Committee to speak publicly. Her concern was the feudal family system, an issue of great controversy. She urged that the Meiji Civil Code of 1898, which governed the rights of family members, be replaced with a democratic family system. Because of the convoluted manner of gaining the floor both in committee and in the general assembly she had to present her views using the required indirect method called interpolation. She had to direct questions to appropriate government ministers as they presented legislation formulated in bureaucratic sessions open only to members of the ruling coalition.

In this roundabout manner Katô spoke to constitutional issues of civil rights. She charged that there was insufficient attention to equal rights for men and women in the draft of Japan's new constitution, and she pointed out that the 1898 Civil Code did not recognize the rights of wives. Her formal question rested on the issue of whether the government would recognize that the feudal practices embedded in the Civil Code conflicted with the democratic changes anticipated in the new constitution; or whether these oppressive laws would be maintained under the guise of traditional and, therefore, good customs. It soon became apparent that Katô was fighting an oppressive system that necessarily subordinated females to male members of a family and to male citizens of the nation. She was concerned that the rights and needs of women and children would not be adequately provided for if the "traditional good custom" of an all-powerful household head remained.

Katô's comments and questions in the Constitution Committee meeting were the focus of the next day's news reporting. Describing her performance, a journalist wrote, "The way in which she [Katô] logically interpolated proved her real sagacity in statesmanship. By so displaying her education and qualifications, she, as a novice, showed that she is not inferior to the male Diet members."

While a new constitution was successfully passed in November 1946, revision of the 1898 Civil Code continued to be hotly debated throughout much of 1947, and a revised Civil Code did not become effective until January 1,

1948. Katô would continue to press the issues of inequality under the family law as it existed in the 1898 Civil Code but would find that she could do so more effectively and openly on radio and in newspapers than in the Diet. During the rest of 1946 and throughout 1947 she insisted in the media that revision of the Civil Code was as important for the future of women as the rewriting of the constitution. The final revision did do away with the legally superior position of men and the subjugation of women within a male-dominated family system as Katô had demanded.

VII

Practicing "Grassroots" Democracy

Election to the Diet had been exhilarating, but Katô Shidzue found that she exercised power more successfully by working outside this male-dominated, conservative institution. In the company of other women she was instrumental in forming political and social action groups, petitioning and rallying the public in support of women's causes, and using the media to publicize women's issues. She also found time to write articles, pamphlets, and her first autobiography in Japanese, all in the service of political goals she hoped to achieve. She was not always successful in her endeavors, but her viewpoints were continuously before the Japanese public and the Americans at SCAP.

Debating Democracy

One major success of 1946, attributable in large measure to Katô Shidzue, was the establishment of an official newspaper for the Women's Democratic Club, *The Women's Democratic Newspaper*. The first issue, launched on August 14, 1946, was four pages long, reported national and international issues of interest to women, and featured local club news. Over the next two years the paper's circulation grew to about sixty-eight thousand, considerably less than the two hundred to two hundred and fifty thousand circulation of the immensely popular and long-established *Young Woman* and *The Housewife's Friend,* but more than many women's magazines that printed in the range of ten to twenty thousand. All newspapers and magazines were limited in both length and distribution by paper shortages, but they were passed along to neighbors and so reached many more women than the official print count would indicate.

The inaugural issue included articles by both Katô and Miyamoto Yuriko. In the issue of October 31, 1946, Katô presented her views on the equality of men and women as set forth in the new constitution. While she clearly believed that with the new constitution women had improved their status, she expressed grave concern that the changes had not gone far enough. She insisted that for real protection of equal rights the Civil Code of 1898 must be substantially revised. As it stood this feudal code supported anti-democratic, prewar relationships which made men legally superior to women and thus contradicted the proposed equality clauses of the postwar constitution, which would guarantee that "all people are equal under the law" and that there should be "no discrimination in political, economic or social relations because of race, creed, sex, social status, or family origin." One would expect Katô's article to be applauded by all members of the Women's Democratic Club as an appropriately liberal interpretation of democracy. It was, however, precisely on this liberalism and the issue of democracy, as Katô defined it, that her long association with Miyamoto Yuriko was sundered.

During the twenties, Katô had met regularly with Miyamoto in different discussion and political groups. At that time they seemed like-minded on issues of women's rights. After Yuriko had traveled to the Soviet Union in 1927, she became committed to a communist vision of social revolution. In 1932 she met and married Miyamoto Kenji, a leader in the illegal Japan Communist Party. They were together only a few months before Yuriko was arrested and Kenji went underground to hide from the police. Soon he, too, was jailed, not to be released until the Americans freed political prisoners in 1945. Yuriko spent several short periods in jail, but was finally released permanently in the late thirties due to deteriorating health. Shidzue recorded in her diary that she met Yuriko again on February 6, 1939, when both women attended a lecture given by a noted wartime economist on Japan's economic position at that time. At that time Shidzue commented that it was not the lecture, but Miyamoto Yuriko's questions afterward, which had caught her attention. She went on to exclaim that of the women of that time Miyamoto was the one who deserved the greatest respect. By fall 1946, however, it was obvious that the political perspectives of these two women had become incompatible.

Their postwar conflict, according to Katô, centered on different interpretations of "democracy." Katô drew on her experiences in America and defined democracy in a liberal fashion endorsing a definition providing for freedom and equality for all members of a society. Miyamoto drew on what she called a "new democracy" exhibited by the pragmatic experiences of the revolutionaries in the USSR and the communists in China, not from the anachronistic interpretations heard in the United States and Europe. She called Katô's vision old-fashioned and bourgeois. Here, in miniature, was the rift between the liberal left and radical left in Japan and the tension that would be known worldwide as the **Cold War.** The division was deep, sides were taken, and by the summer of 1948,

Katô, Akamatsu, Yamamuro, and Yamamoto, along with others, withdrew from the Women's Democratic Club.

Assaults on Women's Rights

Before her days with the club waned, Katô joined with other club members, Diet representatives, and labor union members in an astonishing example of women's solidarity. On November 15, 1946, two women members of the Japan Cinema and Theater Labor Union attended an early evening union meeting in Tokyo. Afterward, about seven P.M. the women walked to the nearby train station. As soon as they passed through the ticket turnstile, they were accosted by American MPs (military police) while a couple of young railway employees looked on. The women pleaded with the Japanese men to help them explain their presence to the MPs, but to no avail, and the MPs forcibly escorted them to a nearby police box. In spite of showing union membership cards, the Japanese police and the MPs assumed the women were prostitutes and took them to Itabashi police station where they joined sixty-eight other women who had been similarly rounded up. Different women were then asked such questions as; "How often have you been brought here? You must have had intercourse with several men. How old are you? It is amazing that you have not had any intercourse until now." (The youngest female brought in was fifteen years old.) Next, the women were trucked against their will to Yoshihara Hospital, where they joined others rounded up throughout Tokyo, thus forming a group of two hundred and seventy. All of the women were forced to undergo venereal disease examinations for which they were required to pay a five-yen fee. By the time the two Cinema and Theater Union women were released it was one A.M. and, since the last trains had stopped for the night, they were permitted to stay until dawn in an unheated room chilled by the night air blowing through the broken windows.

Although this was not the only such incident reported to union leadership and Diet women, it was the most vigorously publicized. Over the next few days detailed articles appeared in women's newspapers, while it was all but ignored in national newspapers. The *Women's Democratic Newspaper* headline read "A Virgin Protests the Round-up of Girls on the Street." Here one union victim told of the pain she and other innocent virgins felt at their treatment by the police. The official excuse was that the police could not determine on the spot just who was and who was not a prostitute. Furthermore, the police said they could not be expected to treat prostitutes as human beings. This seemed a form of barbaric logic to the young woman. The article did not mention the role of the American MPs for it was against SCAP policy to permit any negative reference to the army of occupation. The outcry of this young union member against deprivation of her fundamental human rights was heard loud and clear by Representative Katô and Lt. Weed at CIE. Immediately union representatives, Representative Katô, other Socialist Diet women, the JCP Diet woman, and a few SCAP officials at CIE joined together to carefully investigate the incident.

In an interview at the Government Section of SCAP on November 29, one of the victims stated that "a Reign of Terror for Japanese women had come." In further investigations the Diet women discovered that of seventy women taken to the hospital from Itabashi police station, fewer than ten were found to be identifiable as prostitutes. Union women and men who interviewed the American MPs involved were treated contemptuously, as the MPs declared "You have no right to lodge a protest with us." When the Japanese asked whether their own police should have the right to question the MPs or determine the manner in which women on the streets should be treated, they were told, "The Police are practically incompetent at present. They should follow our orders absolutely. . . . It is up to us to decide how to treat women rounded up. You have no right to say anything about it."

Katô and the other concerned women worked vigorously over a two-week period as they investigated the issues and questioned hospital authorities, local police, MPs, Metropolitan Police Board officials, and others. Their research was detailed and thorough. Katô exerted her influence with Weed and CIE through frequent telephone calls and personal interviews. She also met with officials at the Public Health and Welfare Division and the Policy and Planning Unit in an effort to solve the health problem VD caused without undermining human rights. In the end Katô and the many other women investigating this travesty against women's rights discovered that no one at any of the Japanese or American institutions contacted accepted responsibility for the policy, which led to indiscriminate rounding up of women for VD examinations. The police claimed that the MPs required the Japanese take this action. The hospital spokesman declared he was merely following police orders. SCAP (Provost Marshall, Public Health and Welfare, Government, Public Safety and G-1 Sections) disclaimed responsibility saying that there were no written orders for such a roundup.

Katô and other activist women realized that when they attempted to secure women's rights either by formal methods in bureaucratic or legislative forums, or by informal methods through the offices of SCAP, they could not expect success unless the respective officials approached were in agreement with their goals. Gaining elective office might have given women pride but it had not given them power. Easy entree at SCAP might give the appearance of influence, but it only produced results if powerful officials sanctioned the specific activity or policy. As they had in the past the women determined to use another democratic weapon.

On December 15, 1946, about two thousand women gathered at Dai Ichi Elementary School in Tokyo for a "mass meeting" called by a coalition of sponsors to "demand a halt to alleged indiscriminate rounding up of 'clean working women as well as virgins' in periodic drives against 'street girls' ... (and) to demand police recognition of (women's) civil rights in 'new democratic Japan.'" This "Rally to Protect Women" was sponsored by Katô, JSP associates, JCP women, the Women's Democratic Club, the large umbrella unions of All Japan Federation of Labor and the Congress of Industrial Unions, the New Japan Women's League, the Federation of Cooperative Unions, the Working Women's Union, the National Railway Workers' Union, the All Japan Farmers' Union, the Japan Women's Christian Temperance Union (WCTU), and the Young Communist League. Here was grassroots activism in action.

This rally addressed larger questions than the particular incidents of forced VD examinations; the featured slogan was "down with the Yoshida government." Speeches, reports, and comments placed blame for the policy of indiscriminately rounding up women with the conservative coalition government headed by Yoshida Shigeru, and on the Japanese police. In accordance with SCAP rules prohibiting criticism of any actions taken by the army of occupation, the American authorities and the MPs did not come under fire. The rally became an opportunity for speakers from each organization to decry the discriminatory nature of this specific grievance, the general lack of equality for women it represented, and the travesty this policy made of democracy. Speakers emphasized that actions taken by the police were daily occurrences and that compulsory examinations ignored the human rights of women. Equally important, the speeches emphasized more general problems: the lack of adequate food, rampant inflation, undemocratic actions against village women, the poverty of the working class, the inferior and unequal wage scale for women, and the generally undemocratic actions of the police. Freedom of assembly and the right to petition had been written into the new constitution. These women showed clearly that they recognized the power of these tools of **grassroots democracy.**

"Reverse Course"

On December 17, a larger rally planned by union men took place and shortly thereafter the men called a general strike for February 1, 1947, hoping to bring down the Yoshida government. MacArthur's vehement cancellation of this strike has been considered pivotal to the so-called **reverse course** of the American Occupation. Japanese on the left, like Kanjû and Shidzue, consider this the point at which forward progress of Japan's labor and socialist movements was compromised, and turned back, or "reversed." This strike, the 2/1 Strike, as it is often referred to, is featured in labor, political, and women's histories of the Occupation Period.

By the end of 1946 Japan's economy appeared to be making little headway against the devastation wrought by war and defeat. Inflation continued to rise, living costs increased, wages were held down, and what goods were available were primarily exchanged through the **black market.** At the beginning of this second postwar winter, housing was inadequate, coal for heat was either of uncertain availability or too expensive, and warm clothing and adequate health care were out of the question for many workers. Although union demands for wage increases were fairly modest under the circumstances, they were unacceptable to the government and other employers. The JCP in cooperation with labor union leadership, and, later, the Socialists, determined that the answer was to call a general strike. It would be a strike involving thirty-three unions with a combined membership of six million workers, and it would bring Japan to a halt. MacArthur's forced cancellation of this general strike made it the most famous non-event of the postwar period.

To some the intensification of previous rulings by MacArthur to prevent mass meetings appeared to block the very social advances the Americans had seemed to be fostering in Japan. There was no doubt that it severely reduced labor's power, but it also had an adverse effect on women. As the "Rally to Protect Women" illustrates, women found that in difficult times, when they could not affect policy through either formal or informal power channels, the democratic right to assemble, or in this case to strike, was an important method for gathering support to address grievances and pressure for social change. The suppression of the general strike and MacArthur's anti–mass-meeting policy on which it was based were a setback for grassroots democratic actions by women as well as for the labor movement in general. In later comments Katô Shidzue would refer to MacArthur's action as oppressive and, like others, single it out as a primary cause of the demise of socialist influence.

A Separate Department for Women's Affairs

On April 25, 1947, the second postwar elections for the Diet were held. Both Kanjû and Shidzue ran again and were reelected. This was particularly satisfying for Shidzue as most women elected the previous year lost. Out of eighty-six women candidates only fifteen were elected.

Socialists had been so successful overall that a coalition

government headed by the JSP leader Katayama Tetsu was formed. Although this government, which lasted for only ten months, proved fairly ineffectual, the fact that the Socialists were in positions of importance during the last half of 1947 was helpful to Katô Shidzue and her female JSP colleagues as they fought for a separate national women's bureau. Beginning in March 1946, and for the following eighteen months, Katô met frequently with Ethel Weed and other American officials at CIE and the Government Section to pressure for a cabinet level bureau for women's affairs. Though not the only woman working with SCAP on this issue, Katô was certainly the most frequent and persistent lobbyist, and she was both welcome and effective. No doubt her ability to carry on discussions with Weed and her colleagues in English gave her an important advantage.

At its annual meeting of September 1946 the Socialist Party first took up the issue of a separate women's division. Shidzue presented a draft describing what she saw as the purpose and function of such a department. She also submitted this draft to SCAP officials for review. Shidzue's preamble justified the new department as follows. "It is absolutely necessary for the establishment of a democratic Japan to emancipate women from feudalistic bondage and raise their social status." She went on to say that the nation must not only revise the constitution but also must extensively revise the civil and criminal codes and any other legal statutes that inhibit the full emancipation of women and thus undermine their equal status in society. Consequently there was "a pressing need to set up, at this moment, a strong institute" that would promote women's interests and formulate fundamental policies, provide appropriate facilities, and conduct research into questions affecting women in areas of education, labor, family, law, and nutrition.

Next, Shidzue's draft stressed issues of social education and formal schooling, and provided for the supervision of women's medical colleges and nursing schools. Most important, this new body would oversee the health and welfare of women and children, including medical care and education for women during pregnancy and childbirth. Nationally funded health care was a given. Finally, Shidzue hoped the new department would actively protect women through a more sensitive judicial system, a women's police force, and a family court that would deliberate on the basis of revised statutes guaranteeing women's equal rights. In fact everything mentioned invaded the turf of other cabinet ministries and, consequently, had little hope of being written into law. This document of late September 1946, however, underscored Shidzue's continued anticipation of a democratic revolution for women and children, which would take the form of universal protection of health care and livelihood and expansive social welfare policies. This was why Shidzue was a socialist and why she felt adoption of socialist programs was essential to the achievement of political and economic equality for women in the new democratic Japan.

Strong opposition from all directions for any independent women's department meant that women who favored such an institution had to pressure relentlessly to realize their goal. The issue became a topic for radio discussions and public lectures. The women lobbied in public forums, and in offices of SCAP's Government and CIE sections. Katô was a sponsor of enactment legislation in the House of Representatives, and JSP Senator Akamatsu, after her election, was a sponsor in the House of Councillors. By late spring and early summer of 1947, a women's bureau seemed achievable, though not in the radical configuration Katô had envisioned. The Women's and Minors' Bureau, a sub-section of the Labor Ministry, was established on September 1, 1947. Katô showed her political strength in the struggle to name the bureau's first chief. Her nomination, the socialist Yamakawa Kikue, was appointed.

Reviewing Civil Liberties in the New Japan

The year 1947 was a busy one for Shidzue. In May she and her husband were visited by an old acquaintance, Roger Baldwin, who became the first American civilian without Occupation connections to be permitted to visit Japan. His purpose as director of the **American Civil Liberties Union** (**ACLU**) was to consult with Japanese leaders on the state of civil liberties in Japan. Needless to say his old acquaintances, the Katôs, most especially Shidzue, who could converse easily in English, came immediately to his mind.

Baldwin found that both Shidzue and Kanjû had good words to say for SCAP, though both were willing to criticize certain American-sponsored activities they felt interfered with civil rights. Kanjû, for example, complained that SCAP required five days' notice of meetings and insisted that American MPs and SCAP interpreters be present at all left-wing Socialist meetings. He noted that during the militarist past even the Japanese police had required but a few hours' notice. He went on to criticize MacArthur's halting of the general strike called for February 1st. Kanjû, a strike leader, considered that the labeling of this labor action as a communist adventure was an excuse to break labor's power.

Baldwin spoke at greater length and more frequently with Katô Shidzue, who talked freely and vented some of her frustration over the political injustices she was familiar with as a member of the female minority in both the Socialist Party and the Diet. Overall, she identified bureaucratic arrogance and economic inflation as the two most pressing issues facing Japan. The tenor of her remarks suggested that the bureaucracy was corrupt and that it, as well as all the political parties, had not been adequately purged of fascist wartime leadership. As to rampant inflation and other impoverishing economic issues, she believed "the time (was) ripe for nationalization of key industries, banking first, then coal and fertilizer." She found the twin goals of democratization of unions and political parties still elusive and yet their realization essential if the heralded democratic changes were to be achieved. Although she spoke favorably about SCAP's attempts to secure these ends, she found, for example, that the suppression of the February 1st General Strike "unduly intimidated" the unions and their leadership, and set back the socialist cause. That said, she applauded the action's exposure of the anti-democratic Communists. Her solution to the union problem was to eliminate their political control and permit them to work as "an organic unity," a solution with anarchistic overtones. Obvious in these observations is the fact that at this time Shidzue still hoped for the elusive democratic revolution founded on socialism.

This did not mean, however, that she admired her own Socialist Party. In fact, her remarks about the autocratic internal workings of the Socialist Party were scathing. She said that the party was "dominated by an executive committee elected annually at a convention, and deaf to the voice of the membership, who (were) never consulted on policy or program." She believed that with the premiership in the hands of the socialists it was even more important that "Party rank and file be consulted," but that there was, in fact, "no freedom of speech for Party members." She also blamed the "anti-communist policy of SCAP" for the Americans' determined support of "reactionaries" in both conservative parties and the right wing of the JSP. Even her husband was not exempt from criticism, for she included the entire leadership in her scathing remarks, and implied that all these men were determined to ignore women, who, regardless of visibility, remained categorized with the "rank and file." No one who fell outside her definition of democratic socialist politics escaped her criticism.

In other interviews with Baldwin, Shidzue discussed infringements on the rights of GIs and Japanese women who broke the rules of nonfraternization. The fact that SCAP prevented GIs from marrying Japanese women troubled her, because this policy resulted in many father-less poor children. Furthermore, she expressed a general concern about the lack of birth-control education in Japan, and spoke more specifically about the tragic effect this had on the hundreds of girls pregnant by U.S. GIs who got abortions. This dismayed her, for she was gener-ally opposed to abortion and, most definitely, did not find it appropriate as a birth-control method. She explained that she was in the midst of trying to replace the wartime **Eugenic Protection Laws** with legislation that would emphasize education and the use of contraceptives and consequently make abortion less necessary.

Discord at Home

There were times during these first postwar years that Katô Shidzue had to turn her attention away from politics toward extraordinary family matters. Certainly, at all times she had to look after her young daughter, now a toddler, make sure there was food to eat, and provide any support her husband needed. These were the minimum duties expected of a Japanese wife and mother even in the new democratic Japan. Sometimes, however, as in the fall of 1947, even more was expected. Shidzue's stepdaughter, Sumiko, had turned nineteen in April of that year. Impressed by her parents' associations with Americans and the welcoming manner in which they interacted with members of SCAP, Sumiko did not think it remiss to follow suit. In accordance with her age and interests she began to entertain an American GI.

As Shidzue recounted in 1988, in spite of her own close association with American officials and her longtime affection for America, having a GI hanging around her house was not what she had wanted for Sumiko. She believed her stepdaughter had picked up the wrong signals. "Katô (Kanjû) and I were continuously going back and forth to GHQ, and even though I was a woman, I spoke on equal terms with those in the army of occupation. From Sumiko's point of view this seemed wonderful." She thought her stepmother glamorous because she spoke English and met easily with foreigners; she admired this international ambiance. Sumiko's own manner of entering that world, however, upset Shidzue very much.

One day Shidzue came back to the house and discovered Sumiko and a GI lounging on the sofa together. Shocked, she asked the young man for his superior's name. Her stepdaughter was surprised and hurt. The GI left immediately and Shidzue explained to Sumiko that while the GI was undoubtedly a good person, he was not the sort of person Sumiko should keep company with. She explained further that the elder Katôs' association with the army of occupation was a matter of business. Sumiko might think of her relationship with the GI in a similar way, but, in fact, outsiders would not be so benevolent. There would be gossip; people would speculate about marriage; and Sumiko might act rashly. Shidzue concluded by suggesting that Sumiko was an emotionally inexperienced girl, and a romantic alliance was new and must seem exciting to her, but she must understand her duty and break off this relationship. Shidzue remembered this as a mutually respectful exchange that ended the issue in accordance with parental wishes.

Writing a life story, especially about emotionally entangling events, is a risky matter at best. It is certainly tempting to make sure that all loose ends are tied up and that everyone appears in the best light. Shidzue was writing about a delicate situation from several complex perspectives; her relations with her stepdaughter, her own ability to handle an awkward family situation, her views on fraternization between GIs and Japanese women, her ideas on social class, and her attitudes toward the army of occupation. It is not surprising, then, that she would gloss over the rough edges of this incident. There is, however, a differently remembered description of this event, one which places it in a more probing light. This version is probably misremembered to some extent, as well. Certainly the quoted dialogue, which was in some cases secondhand, could not be exact. This version was published in 1951, just four years after the confrontation.

The second account is provided by the wife of an army colonel, who joined her husband in Tokyo in August 1947. That fall she met Katô Shidzue personally, and a short time later heard her as the featured speaker at a University Club meeting. Shidzue, "Mrs. S." in the text, "was a slim, straight woman in a blue kimono, with good eyes and a determined chin. She'd spoken about her experience as one of the first women elected to the Diet. . . . Throughout the evening, she'd shown much intelligence but little warmth of personality. That might well be her public manner, I thought. When she came to our house I found that Mrs. S.'s private manner was just the same. She sat very erect in our living room, her social mask carefully adjusted." The military wife was not sympathetic to Shidzue's public or private demeanor.

The meeting at the colonel's house was officially related to quelling noise from a nearby dance club, the "Bombshell"; but Shidzue had something more important on her mind. She asked if the colonel might intercede for her on a personal matter. She then told about a GI who was coming to her house every night, walking on the *tatami* mats in his shoes and making a general nuisance of himself. Her daughter had the idea that this young man was going to marry her. Shidzue is quoted as saying, "One night I came home late from a meeting, and there he was, lying on the mats with his bottle of Suntory (whiskey). I asked him not to come so often. He said he'd come any time he chose. *Who* won the war? *Who* attacked Pearl Harbor? His language was very abusive." She then asked for help. She did not want public attention drawn to this situation; her name already appeared frequently in the newspapers. She asked the colonel to speak privately with the young man's commanding officer, which he did. The commanding officer, in turn, spoke with the GI who assured him that he would never go back there. Speaking quite rudely about Shidzue he added, "Most of the time she's out gadding around. I told her once she oughta stay home and take better care of her daughter." He then admitted that he had been drinking too much lately. "Ordinarily, I'm the quiet kind. But as soon as I take a drink, my brain starts buzzing and I lose my inhibitions." Then, after assuring the commanding officer that he had not compromised the daughter, the soldier was admonished to stay away from this girl and the matter was ended.

This was a more serious incident than Shidzue wanted to admit. Even her version shows a personal, if abbreviated, look at the emotional conflicts that necessarily accompanied private interactions with the army of occupation. There is also some indication of Shidzue's attitudes about social class in both versions of the event. She was all in favor of GI marriages with Japanese girlfriends when she discussed the subject dispassionately with Roger Baldwin, but she was much too savvy about the realities of young, impressionable, well-bred Japanese girls dazzled by the apparent wealth and sophistication of American GIs to let such a romantic encounter ruin her own stepdaughter's life. Social democracy had its place in the new Japan, and revolutionary changes were to be welcomed to a large extent, but there was a limit to what could be tolerated on the personal level. This illustrious family must be protected from the tragedies Shidzue had observed in the new democracy.

VIII

Enduring Political Reversals

By 1949 it appeared to Katô Shidzue that her country was suffering from a postwar American Occupation that had gone on too long. She also felt that her compatriots had failed to take up the important causes of social welfare they had so readily embraced just after the war. She still maintained her belief in social democracy and her determination that women should share in its fruits. Women had gained political equality through the new constitution and with the new family code in place, they no longer could be legally oppressed by male members of their family. There was, however, a great chasm between rights as expressed in documents and actual practice in political, economic, and social arenas. Katô saw her dreams of women's liberation from economic want and personal misery slipping away. She redoubled her efforts for her twin goals of personal and public rights for women.

A Fight for Family Planning

That same summer Shidzue began working toward revision of the 1941 National Eugenic Law with eight other JSP female members in the House of Representatives, and the two women Socialist Party members in the House of Councillors. While, in general, male JSP members could not be counted on to vote for women's issues any more frequently than conservatives, a handful of men, most prominently Ôta Tenrei, joined in this effort. The timing of this campaign seemed auspicious. SCAP's health officials were calling on the nation to recognize the severity of Japan's population pressures and take appropriate measures. Also, the country's economic conditions had not improved much over the two years since the end of the war, and the basic necessities of food, clothing, and shelter continued to be difficult to secure. Finally, the sitting coalition government was headed by a socialist, as were several cabinet ministries, and Socialist Diet members held a plurality in both houses.

On August 28, 1947, a Eugenic Protection Law was introduced in the House of Representatives by Katô Shidzue, and two other JSP representatives, the physician, Ôta Tenrei, and Fukuda Masako, a colleague in the JSP Women's Section. This was not the bill that Shidzue had wanted, for it contained significant provisions for abortion, which she opposed, and no provisions for birth-control clinics or education, which she believed vital. The abortion clauses were supported by physicians, however, who, Shidzue explained, had seen the economic pressures of housing and food that drove women to desperation. She had to agree with her physician colleagues that a medically obtained legal abortion would be preferable to the more dangerous alternatives in practice at the time. The scholar Samuel Coleman has described the situation at this time.

> [P]ressed by stringent economic conditions and lacking the means to control conception, [the women] sought ways to end their unwanted pregnancies. Perhaps because of the atmosphere of thriving black markets, physicians were no longer threatened by the law against abortions; not only were the Ob–Gyns providing them, but other

physicians and even veterinarians began performing abortions on a regular basis. In consequence, rates for infanticide and infant abandonment rose to their highest level in postwar Japan between 1945 and 1950, nearly trebling their 1940 level.

Unfortunately the bill was permitted to die with the close of this lackluster legislative session at the end of the year. Socialist Party Prime Minister Katayama had proved a strikingly incapable leader. Many significant legislative issues essential to the economic well-being of the impoverished nation were at a standstill. While the legislators argued over bills fundamental to industrial and agricultural recovery, the people continued to suffer daily. Workers' wages were not keeping up with the rampant inflation. A report of July 1947 stated that a Tokyo family earned about 2756 yen per month and had to spend 2930 yen to live, three-quarters of it in the black market. Industrial production continued to rise at a slow rate and the trade deficit grew daily. Many essential goods were simply not available, and the food crisis would not go away. The Katayama government seemed unable to progress on any of these major issues. SCAP tried to get the Diet to legislate wage and price controls, rationing, and equitable distribution of the essential goods that were available. No such laws were forthcoming. In fact, the Diet deadlocked on budget legislation, basic to even the most modest level of government operations. The budget was still being debated as late as November. SCAP's reverse course on Japan's social and economic trajectory combined with Katayama's incompetence and the Socialists' lack of a majority to bring government to a virtual standstill.

Shidzue, a member of the Budget Committee, used her right of interpolation during one of the committee meetings to ask Prime Minister Katayama about his position on birth control. She posed her question within the context of the economic costs of Japan's dramatic population increase. Her purpose was to obtain a public statement from Katayama for the record. The prime minister admitted that the nation's sudden population increase was serious and required attention. He stated frankly that the government was "so preoccupied with urgent economic and political problems that it [could] not propose concrete plans for overseas emigration or for the popularization of birth control methods." In fact, while the government might be "preoccupied," it was doing nothing.

On March 10, the Katayama government was replaced by another coalition government, this time headed by the Democratic Party leader, Ashida Hitoshi. The new cabinet included eight socialists, one of whom was Katô Kanjû as Minister of Labor. This time Katô Shidzue and her like-minded associates decided to give a Democratic Party senator in the House of Councillors the responsibility for introducing the birth-control bill. The draft stated, "The aims of this law are to protect the life and health of mothers, to prevent the increase of inferior progeny and in consequence to contribute to physical improvement in the nation."

Once again this was a eugenics bill, directed at genetic improvement of the Japanese people. It was not the bill for family planning that Shidzue had wanted, but it was the best that could be hoped for within the legislative climate of the moment. The bill's twenty-three articles described and defined the appropriate instances for voluntary sterilization, compulsory sterilization, physicians' required reports and prohibitions, temporary contraception, interruption of pregnancy (abortion), penal regulations, and nullification of the current law. The bill became law in July 1947.

Katô Shidzue was not proud of the legislation. She had wanted a law that would stress education and birth control. The Socialist Party Women's Affairs Section had placed a high priority on nationwide clinics that would provide information for women on all aspects of family planning, similar to the sort of clinic Shidzue had opened in Tokyo in 1937. Not only were such educational organizations missing in this law, the only mention of birth control came in Chapter Five, which spoke of "temporary contraception." Only a certified physician could prescribe "measures for temporary contraception," although "every one is free to apply such measures to himself or herself." Education about birth control would be discouraged. On the other hand, there were cases in which abortion, again performed by a specially licensed physician, could be provided: in the case of a pregnancy or delivery that would endanger the life of the mother, and in the case of rape, and some instances of hereditary disease or mental illness. In 1949 the law was amended to include a vague clause giving a designated physician supervised by a local review committee the right to recommend abortion for women who proved debilitating economic or physical circumstances, and a clause about clinics for "eugenic education" or marriage counseling. Certain offices could also propagate and provide guidance "concerning the proper method of conception adjustment."

From 1949, Japanese women increased their dependency on abortion as their primary birth-control method. This was a great disappointment to Shidzue. She believed that the law she had worked hard for had become primarily an opportunity for physicians to enrich themselves, for the clause which required that only designated physicians could legally perform abortions guaranteed a lucrative practice for a few doctors. It is no wonder that physicians had backed the original law, and that even today attempts to alter this moneymaking provision for physicians have not been possible.

Elective Reversals

The general election held on January 23, 1949, was a blood bath for the JSP. The number of JSP representatives dropped from one hundred and forty-three to forty-eight. Both Katôs lost, a terrible blow. When Shidzue ran again it was for a seat in the House of Councillors in 1950. Kanjû did not have a chance to return to the Diet until the next election for the **Lower House,** held in October 1952. At that time he left his district in Aichi Province and ran for his wife's old seat in a heavily left-wing district of Tokyo and won.

After the 1949 election was over Shidzue wrote an eight-page analysis of the Socialist Party defeat for Ethel Weed at CIE. In it she stated that the most important reason the public voted against the Socialist Party was the inadequate attention the party had paid to educating the people about socialist principles. Second, the party was torn by factionalism which reflected prewar differences that had been ignored by those determined to establish a larger, more powerful postwar party. Third, the public believed that the party had not followed through on its promised program. Here Shidzue commented that the Socialists had been undermined by the ideological and programmatic compromises they had made in their attempts to cooperate with nonsocialist parties. Furthermore, SCAP had prevented the JSP from implementing their own programs. She believed that the ideals of socialist policies clashed with the reality of SCAP's directives. Under the circumstances "the Party's cooperation with Occupation policies in the name of the Japanese Government totally lost the support . . . of the Japanese masses." Fourth, "[t]he Party failed to control the bureaucratic forces" which must be considered a "great menace" to the democratization of Japan. "These rotten irresponsible bureaucrats hampered the advancement of renovating policies. One of the reasons why the Party gave the impression of betraying its promises must be attributed to the resistance made from inside the administration." Finally the public expected too much of the Socialist Party. It was caught between its desires to implement socialist programs and its "responsibility to practice Occupation policies."

Shidzue had begun to question the usefulness of working so closely with the discredited Occupation authorities. The democratic revolution that she and others believed would follow the tragedy of war had been turned back by the political and economic "reverse course" instituted by both the Americans and the Japanese conservatives who dominated the government. Bureaucrats of both nations had stopped the forward movement of democratic socialism, she believed.

Why had the conservative Democratic/Liberal Parties been so successful at this time, she asked? The primary reason, she believed, was the popularity of the Liberal leader, Yoshida Shigeru, and the fact that party members had campaigned against the Occupation. She pointed out, "Cooperating attitudes toward the Occupation Forces are becoming quite unpopular among the Japanese People. They support the action or speeches [of those] who pretend to ignore the fact of unconditional surrender." Yoshida and his party promised the people a free economy, a better life, lower taxes, reduced rationing, and other fine-sounding general palliatives. This was what the people wanted to hear.

The JCP also had gained stature from their anti-American stance. In fact, Shidzue admired the Communist Party's successful use of publicity. They had their own daily paper and several periodicals and they received positive support from intellectuals in literary fields while these same people criticized the Socialists. Communists stayed close to the lower classes, the working people. They set up offices where these people could come and consult about tax problems or express other concerns. They helped people to fight landlords, welcomed repatriated soldiers home, entertained children, taught young people to dance and so forth, while the Socialists isolated themselves in the government. What use is it, she seemed to ask, to appear powerful, if you don't apply that power with the good of the people in mind?

The Peculiarities of Japan's Political Parties

At the end of 1945 it had seemed to the politically astute Katôs that a democratic revolution was inevitable and that they would both participate in its realization. For the first two years of the Occupation they believed that the Americans were supporting the political goals of their Socialist Party. This belief began to fade with the onset of the "reverse course" in 1947 and accelerated downward with the 1949 election debacle. What had happened? Shidzue blamed the Socialist Party's decline on both the Occupation, which had switched its political support from the Socialists to the Democratic-Liberal Parties, or conservatives, and on the Socialist Party, which had praised occupation policies long after the Americans had ceased to back the JSP.

To a great extent these social and political reversals reflected the larger events occurring in the Far East. In 1949 Mao Tse-tung's (Mao Zedong) Communist Party in China defeated Chang Kai-shek's Nationalists and formed the People's Republic of China. This action brought the **Cold War**'s powerful presence to the Far East and made the American government more attentive to what was happening in Japan. Occupation authorities, once again, moved to bolster the conservative cause as they encouraged the "**red purge**" during which many union leaders, left-wing government officials, and teachers were persecuted and lost their jobs. At the same time the Americans initiated discussions toward encouraging the Japanese government to amend the 1947 Constitution by eliminating the famous article that renounced war and prohibited the raising of a military. The American goal was rearmament for its newly discovered ally. Occupation officials appeared to be abandoning their liberal and democratic policies of the early years. It is no wonder that those on the left who had supported the Americans were losing ground to Yoshida and the conservatives, who manipulated the foreign overlords, using SCAP when needed to get rid of the "reds" and standing their ground against SCAP when rearmament was the issue.

American policy, however, was not the whole story. As Shidzue's scathing criticism of her party's leadership suggests, the socialists acted in self-destructive ways. After the war the prewar right and left wings of the socialist movement joined. It was never a happy union. The struggle between these factions meant that social and economic programs often took a back seat to power struggles among the party leadership and the leadership of their associated unions. Kanjū, a powerful left-wing leader with union ties, operated successfully in this atmosphere, enjoying the infighting. Shidzue was much more concerned about social welfare for women and children and countrywide political changes that would lead to national rather than individual capitalist control of major industries, transportation systems, and utilities. Achieving such changes was the reason she had looked forward to a democratic revolution. She had expected her version of democratic socialism would be brought about by the election of representatives who would champion the less fortunate in Japanese society, particularly women. She dreamed of the enactment of socialist programs that would provide safety nets for the poor, the workers, the wives, the children. A social welfare state, akin to the Scandinavian societies of today, not a communist state was her goal. She was not interested in personal party power, but was angered by the party's subordination of Socialist Party Diet women, and therefore the suppression of the needs of their constituents to last place in party discussions.

The 1949 Socialist Party defeat meant the end of any significant socialist power in Japan's government. The Yoshida Democratic-Liberal Coalition was strong and the new **Liberal Democratic Party (LDP)** that was formed from its parts in 1955 was so strong that this political party held control continuously until 1993, and then only lost power for a brief period of time. In 1960 the two factions of the Socialist Party split for good, with the more powerful Japan left-wing Socialist Party vying for elective support with the right-wing, Democratic Socialist Party. While Katô Shidzue remained in the JSP, it became more for voter recognition and to support her husband than as a foundation for her political thinking. In the future she would ignore party labels as she practiced a less conventional form of politics.

Economic Hardship

Katô's bitterness over her own defeat, the Socialist Party's defeat, and what she saw as betrayal by her American allies was devastating. Just the same, the lost election did not mean that she must retire from public service. She expected to work for a Socialist Party renewal and to continue her own activities on selected political and social issues. She would have more time to devote to birth-control education and to her birth-control popularization society, not quite two years old. More and more she began to go her own way. She used her association with the socialists when that was helpful; she sided with conservative officials when that suited her purpose.

In December 1949, Katô captured the harshness of life in Japan and highlighted her own discouragement in letters to America. "It seems to me that people here are spiritually very low compared to pre-war times. They can't dance to the piper's flute! People are depressed and struggling hard trying to cope with deflation and heavy taxation. Working people have to spend all their income for nothing but food and carfare in order to work. Deflation is just as bad as inflation for those who have no savings. I realized that when women do not have an excess of energy to think about tomorrow, being obliged to live only for today, they cannot be intelligent enough to think about family planning."

Katô also brought her friends up to date on family news. Her daughter, Taki, who would be five in March and, admittedly, looked more like a granddaughter, brought her great comfort and joy. Her son, Arata, now just past thirty, was also living at home. He worked at CIE and studied in his spare time. He was responsible for his father, Ishimoto Keikichi, who had returned home from Beijing, China, as a refugee. She added that Arata should have been anticipating a large estate from his grandfather, but Keikichi had lost it all through frivolous and imprudent financial decisions. Arata was still single because his impoverished circumstances precluded any possibility of marriage.

In other letters Shidzue revealed some of the family's material worries. "I feel shame in asking you this, but there are a number of things that our family needs. If you feel that you can spare some of the things listed below, it will be most appreciated by me." She said little Taki needed underwear, knitted things, all sorts of clothes and coats, adding that she was "a rather large size for her age." Shidzue, herself, needed suits, overcoats, sweaters, or just about anything that would fit her and the household needed sheets, bed covers, pillow cases, towels. The family would be happy with discards.

Times that were difficult for everyone in 1949 were made worse in February of that year with the arrival of Joseph M. Dodge, president of a bank in Detroit, as advisor to Prime Minister Yoshida. Dodge recommended that Japan bring inflation under control by balancing the budget through tax increases and price and wage controls. It was a deflationary program that would cause the already squeezed population increased hardship. He expected this and pointed out at a SCAP meeting that "[a] mild increase in unemployment will. . . lead to increased efficiency of labor and a greater production and productivity which makes possible continued volume production at lower prices." Who would buy this increased volume of goods given the low wages and rising unemployment? Dodge expected to increase exports that would help balance the budget. And what about the necessary depression of an already low standard of living? "[The] standard of living has probably been permitted to go too high—cannot increase further—we can't give them everything they want," Dodge reasoned. "It is a tough job to halt a Santa Claus economy." Few Japanese would have recognized their country in this description. Most people felt they were living on the edge of a precipice, and further cuts in their meager livelihood would force them to jump. Unfortunately, unlike Katô Shidzue, not many had friends in America who might help them muddle through the difficult deflationary times.

During the same winter of 1949, another advisor arrived in Tokyo to research Japan's population increase and its inevitable pressure on economic resources. Dr. Warren S. Thompson, Director of the Scripps Foundation for Research in Population Problems, began his temporary mission as technical consultant to SCAP's Natural Resources Section. The report of his findings, made public in March, emphasized the necessity of a comprehensive birth-control program to curb the predicted population explosion that was well underway. He insisted that limitation of births was fundamental to Japan's future survival.

General MacArthur Versus Margaret Sanger

It was within this context of concern over population

growth that Katô Shidzue saw the return of Margaret Sanger to Japan as the perfect rallying point for a nation-wide campaign for birth-control education. She believed that the various pronouncements in favor of a population policy provided a positive environment in which her own program could grow. Publicity from a nationwide Sanger tour and the continued magic of the Sanger name would help to popularize Katô's family-planning program over those emphasizing eugenics or genetic improvement of the nation's people.

On June 28, 1949, Katô wrote Sanger detailing plans for her visit. To maximize publicity and provide adequate financial backing for large public meetings throughout Japan, she had approached Baba Tsunego, president of the *Yomiuri Newspaper,* who had accepted complete responsibility and agreed to issue the invitation. He sent a letter to Sanger setting forth the purpose of the tour: "[to] assist in improving and guiding birth control and sex education in Japan." He went on to outline current population pressures, and state that Sanger's ideas "would be of great help for the reconstruction of a peaceful and cultured nation." He seemed to take SCAP's cooperation for granted. "Mrs. Katô approached SCAP officials for an understanding," he assured Sanger, "and at the same time the Chief Cabinet Secretary and high officials of the Welfare Ministry have promised their support for this end."

Meanwhile the Japanese continued to legislate, editorial-ize, and propagandize favorably for population limitation through birth control. Katô addressed these issues in her birth-control society; the husband and wife team, the Doctors Amano, discussed the issues in their Japan Birth Control Institute; Dr. Majima Kan fostered these ideas in his Japan Birth Control League; and others followed along in several newly formed groups. Simultaneously, representatives of the Catholic Church stepped up their campaign against birth control, but focused their attacks on the Thompson report and SCAP rather than on the activities of Japanese citizens. Catholic opposition was proclaimed by the American missionary Father William A. Kaschmitter, director of the official Catholic newspaper *Tosei News,* the American Catholic Chaplains of Tokyo-Yokohama, The American Catholic Women's Club of Tokyo, American Catholics in the United States, and representatives of the 125,000 Japanese Catholics. On July 1 a spokesman for the pope issued a statement alleging that Occupation authorities were encouraging the Japanese Diet to pass legislation legalizing abortion and permitting the manufacture and sale of contraceptives. "No matter who is responsible for these laws, our Christianity cannot tolerate this barbarous manner of solving a problem, no matter how crucial it can be," the Vatican statement insisted.

Unable to hide from the discussion any longer, on July 2 the supreme commander, General MacArthur, made public a letter he had written to the Tokyo Allied Catholic Women's Club. In it he answered their request that he address the issues raised in population-control reports and their request that he separate the American Occupation from any conclusions favoring the use of abortion and/or contraception. MacArthur did exactly that. "In order to prevent any misunderstanding and to eradicate any misconception, the Supreme Commander wishes it understood that he is not engaged in any study or consideration of the problem of Japanese population control. Such matter does not fall within the prescribed scope of the Occupation and decisions thereon rest entirely with the Japanese themselves." In effect MacArthur disavowed the Thompson report and similar reports by other Occupation advisors; and, in an about-face, removed the entire question of population control and family planning from the Occupation's mission. One aspect of this discussion that was kept from the public's view, however, was that MacArthur also scuttled the proposed Sanger visit; she was denied a visa.

MacArthur's actions were predicated on his ambitions for the future. He was considered a great war hero and successful in his administration of the Occupation of Japan up to this point. The American public, who had wanted to punish the Japanese, were not sympathetic to their economic misery. On the other hand, Americans were impressed with the apparent smooth running of the defeated nation by the supreme commander. MacArthur, basking in this glory, looked to the 1952 U.S. elections and a place at the head of the Republican ticket. He did not want to offend American Catholics with overt support of Japanese population-control policies. Even more definite was his determination to keep the controversial Sanger out of his territory. He certainly had no need of an American birth-control advocate publicizing her views throughout the land to the delight of both the Japanese and American press. Once again, policy decisions emanating from the highest office of the American Occupation short-circuited social democratic progress in Katô Shidzue's new Japan.

IX

Seeking Social Justice at Home and Abroad

In early spring of 1950 Katô Shidzue agreed to run under the JSP banner for a seat in the House of Councillors. Once again her platform focused on family planning. She was still not satisfied with the Eugenics Law and hoped to gain support for additional revisions that would encourage government financing of birth-control education and the distribution of contraceptives to poor women, thereby making abortion less necessary. Her primary concern had always been the health and welfare of mothers and children and the right of women to make their own health and parenthood choices. Here would be a new platform from which to proclaim these principles.

In this second postwar upper-house election half of the seats would be contested, and of these, fifty would be filled by candidates running at-large nationally. The rest would be filled by successful local candidates from prefectural constituencies. To run at-large a candidate needed either strong party backing or the backing of a powerful independent organization, and nationwide name recognition. The competition was not simply among candidates of different parties, but all candidates running for the fifty seats.

Each voter was allowed just one vote; the fifty candidates with the highest vote total would take seats. Katô ran at-large, received the sixth highest vote total nationally, and came in first for the Socialist Party. Her political career was on the move once more; she was elated.

It was an exciting time. The United States and most of her World War II allies, except the USSR, were negotiating a peace treaty for Japan that would officially end the war and give Japan back her sovereignty. But it was also a sobering time. There were still many problems to solve at home as Japan continued to sink deeper into an economic abyss. Katô was a Socialist Party senator, a member of the minority party, in a conservative Yoshida Shigeru government. Just the same she had proved she could command a large nationwide elective base and so could expect to participate vigorously as political control was returned to Japan. She believed that she would have some say in the direction of an all-Japanese controlled program for economic recovery. What she did not yet realize was that cataclysmic events in the Far East would catapult both the new senator and her nation into the international arena as well.

While Katô was still savoring her recent election victory, Japan was brought acutely into international focus when, on June 25, 1950, hostilities broke out in the Korean Peninsula. Fighting began at the 38th parallel, the World War II dividing line between North and South Korea, and immediately escalated into a U.S.-led, United Nations/South Korean war against North Korea and its USSR and Chinese supporters. Here was the Cold War heated up. Given Japan's geographical proximity to Korea, and the American troops stationed in Japan and on the U.S.-controlled island of Okinawa, Japan was forced to be a player in this confrontation. Yoshida's stubborn defense of the postwar Constitution meant that military involvement was not an option. Japan would not change the constitution that their enemy had written for them. Japan, however, would benefit from their crucial location. The Americans would buy all sorts of military material from Japanese factories. The war saved Japan economically. She finally began to recover from the destruction and devastation of World War II. The Korean War, "the forgotten war" as it is often called in America, provided the base on which Japan built its future economic success and its political conservatism. Japan's unexpected thrust into international politics carried Senator Katô Shidzue with it and provided the arena for what she considered her finest hour.

Embracing a New Ideology

Katô Shidzue's dismay over the direction democracy had taken in postwar Japan, her disappointments at her party's ineffectiveness, and her decreased influence at SCAP in the early fifties, all caused her to yearn for a new perspective. Like so many on the left, in the early fifties she suffered a profound loss of faith in the direction her nation was moving. For some activists this meant retreat and isolation, for others greater radicalism outside traditional political party structures, for yet others intellectual submersion and theoretical discussion divorced from action. Shidzue had never been a philosophical theorist; she did not write tracts about her thinking; she believed in action based on an intuitive interpretation of what she thought was right and just. Consequently, in those days of confusion and disappointment she became receptive to a belief system that seemed to solve personal and global problems simply. The organization that appeared to answer her needs was **Moral Re-Armament (MRA),** which professed an ideological framework that was international in focus, aggressively anti-communist, and American in concept and sympathy.

By late 1949 many Japanese, including Shidzue, had become increasingly concerned about the destructive role they saw international communism playing in a precarious world of superpowers and emerging third-world nations. The outbreak of the Korean War confirmed their alarm, causing disruption on the political left. Although Shidzue had identified herself with left-wing socialist causes all of her adult life, she was never supportive of radical visions, and openly opposed communism. Therefore, it is not out of character that Shidzue, a strong Americanophile, and a democratic humanist with European/American philosophical underpinnings, would be attracted to a community of anti-communists in the early fifties. Circumstances dictated that the organization which found her was Moral Re-Armament. During her first intensive encounter with this organization in the summer of 1951, Shidzue concluded that the program preached by MRA's leader, Dr. Frank Buchman, with its internationalist drive for peace, moral framework opposed to communism, and individual preparation for ethical leadership, coincided with her own ideals.

Frank Buchman was an American from Pennsylvania who had begun his adult life as a Lutheran minister. After being forced out of his church position, in the 1920s he founded an organization based on Christian evangelism but not connected with any religious denomination. The group was known during the 1920s and 1930s variously as the Oxford Group and Buchmanites. The "groupers," as they were called, were primarily middle-class British and Americans. Just before World War II the organization's name was changed to Moral Re-Armament, or MRA. After the war the leadership under Buchman's direction modulated its close association with Christianity to make MRA more palatable to Asians and Africans, and embraced an ideology that provided a counterpoint to what they termed the destructive belief of communism. The goals and ideological tenets of MRA were designed to attract political, business, and labor leaders in countries throughout the world who would attend training sessions at MRA-owned facilities, where they would receive guidance toward personal "life-change." These leaders would then guide others toward the ultimate goal of worldwide moral rearmament and the defeat of communism. The organization was most successful in Britain, Germany, Japan, and America and reached its height during the anti-communist cold war years of the fifties and early sixties. When Buchman died in 1961 no single individual was anointed to take his place and by the late sixties, the organization had lost almost all of its strength and audience.

During the summer of 1950 a group of postwar Japanese political, labor, and business leaders were authorized to join an international meeting at MRA headquarters in Caux, Switzerland. There was a flood of applications. This was the first opportunity Japanese had to leave the country since the Occupation began. The group, as it was finally constituted, included the Christian Socialist, ex-Prime Minister Katayama Tetsu, and Sohma Yukika, daughter of the venerated twentieth-century statesman, Ozaki Yukio, and a good friend of Katô Shidzue. The trip coincided with the outbreak and first months of the Korean War, and the Japanese delegates emphasized MRA's fundamental, ideological opposition to the thinking which they felt had brought this war about. In an address before the U.S. Senate a representative of Japan's prime minister stated, "The lawless aggression in Korea is again involving America in great sacrifices. We Japanese wholeheartedly support the action taken by the United Nations and pay high respect to the courageous leadership of President Truman in this matter." He then praised MRA as the truly democratic ideology that would be "the powerful answer to Communism." On August 6, the fifth anniversary of the bombing of Hiroshima, delegate Sohma Yukika spoke to the Americans. "The world does not look to America only for material aid, but also for spiritual leadership. . . . We are so grateful to you for bringing Moral Re-Armament to Japan. . . . We women of Japan wish to do our best to bring this spirit to our country and through her change to the world, because we believe this is the only expression of restitution for her past wrongs, and with this ideology we can build a new world." It was, therefore, the combination of Shidzue's intimate friendship with Sohma Yukika, her open admiration of America, and MRA's anticommunist thrust and international framework that caused her to embrace this ideology one year later. MRA, as she interpreted it, would provide the moral underpinnings for the rest of Katô's public career and personal life.

"Life-Change"

Shidzue's initial interest in MRA was somewhat cynically related to her quest for a visa and funding to travel abroad. Her application to become a delegate to the June 1951 MRA World Assembly on Mackinac Island, Michigan, was approved immediately by the MRA leadership, but held up by Occupation authorities. By this time General MacArthur had been dismissed by President Truman over insubordinate actions in the Korean War. Presumably, his replacement, General Matthew Ridgeway, did not have any prejudices against this Japanese birthcontrol advocate. Just the same obtaining a visa from GHQ was touch and go. She did finally receive a visa, but later than the other delegates and had to travel alone, arriving after the conference opened on June 1.

Mackinac Island in upper Michigan was rich in natural beauty, unique in its rustic, turn of the century atmosphere, and quiet, with a few horse-drawn carriages replacing banned cars. Accommodations at the Grand Hotel were magnificent compared with economically pinched Tokyo, and the food plentiful, varied, and excellent. This experience should have been completely relaxing; in fact it was most intense.

Shidzue listened fervently to Buchman describing early postwar MRA meetings at Caux in which the Germans and French frankly discussed their wartime animosities. She was thrilled by the wonder of these enemies coming together in friendship and understanding. Of particular import to her was the story of the French Socialist leader, Madame Irène Laure, who had been a member of the underground during World War II and whose son had been tortured by Germans. This influential Frenchwoman's hatred of Germany had known no bounds, and yet at Caux, she had become reconciled with her enemies. In fact she "apologized to the Germans for having willed the total destruction of their country." That she was a socialist, a woman, a grieving mother, and a victim of German atrocities, and yet was able to seek unity with her enemy impressed Shidzue. MRA had changed Madame Laure's life and the lives of others, including the famous postwar German leader Konrad Adenauer, and had moved these leaders to a higher plane of public service and personal fulfillment. Shidzue was eager to experience such a change in her own life.

The speakers from other Asian countries, particularly Korea, affected Shidzue most fervently. She began to understand and sympathize with colonial peoples, most especially those who had been oppressed by the Japanese. When the Korean speaker told how his people were not permitted by their Japanese rulers to study or publicly use their own language, and were considered impure and inferior by their oppressors, she was brought to tears. She experienced the same emotions when the delegates from Taiwan, Singapore, and the Malay Peninsula spoke. When Senator Katô responded, she spoke purposefully, apologizing on behalf of her whole nation to those who had been brutalized by the Japanese, and resolved to work for reconciliation with these peoples.

Accepting without compromise the four tenets of Buchman's teachings—absolute honesty, absolute integrity, absolute unselfishness, and absolute love—Shidzue experienced a "religious conversion." Meetings took the form of small-group discussions, or "sharing and guidance" sessions, in which about thirty participants from all over the world gave brief speeches and responses. Sharing was akin to confessing sins and guidance was assumed to come from god as interpreted by MRA leaders.

An International Player

Toward the end of August, Shidzue joined an MRA group that traveled to Europe and then returned to San Francisco in September, arriving at the same time as the Japanese and Allied delegations to the Peace Treaty Conference. This was especially fortuitous for the Socialist Party. The treaty-signing conference included delegates from fifty-two nations pledged to sign a previously negotiated document. Prime Minister Yoshida Shigeru represented Japan, and all Japanese delegates were conservatives. The coincidental arrival of the MRA group meant that JSP members, ex-Prime Minister Katayama Tetsu, Senator Katô Shidzue, and Representative Toganô Satoko were all in the audience as observers.

One reason no JSP delegates had been invited to the conference was that the party's left and right wings could not agree on a response to the treaty's provisions. Yoshida, who did not want to delay the treaty, simply ignored both factions. The Peace Treaty had two major provisions: first, it ended the war and returned sovereignty over Japan to her own people; second, the added Security Agreement, urged on Japan by the Americans in light of the Korean War and the Cold War, instituted a mutual security pact between the United States and Japan. The second provision gave the U.S. government the right to maintain bases in Japan for the purposes of protecting Japan from both external attack and internal disturbances. The JSP left wing vowed to vote against the entire document when it came before the Diet the following month. The right wing was willing to vote for the Peace Treaty provisions, despite what they considered harsh reparations added in San Francisco, but were adamantly opposed to the Security Agreement, which they felt limited Japan's sovereignty.

Ordinarily the left wing could count on Katô Shidzue's vote in the House of Councillors and the right wing would have Toganô Satoko's vote in the House of Representatives. The two women had been adversaries throughout their Diet careers and their votes on issues that split the JSP canceled each other. In fact the two women had become close friends on this trip, and Katô, in keeping with her newly learned behaviors of reconciliation and her strong anti-communist stance, joined Toganô and the right wing to vote for the Peace Treaty but against the Security Agreement. On October 26 both sections of the document were passed in a special session of both houses, though by different margins representing the JSP split. This vote was further evidence that Shidzue's summer of MRA training had changed her politically as well as personally.

MRA began substantively to influence both Shidzue and Kanjû's international activities. In 1954 Kanjû was one of four Japanese delegates in a multinational MRA group who visited Taiwan and the Philippines, countries that retained a strong hatred for the Japanese from their periods of occupation. This mission was seen by the private Japanese delegation as an opportunity to apologize for their nation's wartime atrocities. Later, Kanjû joined an international delegation to South America. In August 1955, Shidzue joined what she called "a taskforce of MRA statesmen" on a mission dedicated to spreading the MRA message to South Asia, the Middle East, and Africa. She was proud to be a member of an international delegation from twenty-six nations.

In between trips abroad both Katôs spread the MRA message from home. For example, they wrote letters of good will to other nationals, especially those in countries which had experienced the brutal hand of the Japanese military and/or occupation administrators before and during the war. Perhaps the most sensitive manifestation of this gesture was their personal message sent to the (South) Koreans in December 1955, in which they apologized on behalf of the Japanese people for Japan's wrongdoing in the past and pledged that they personally would work devotedly for reconciliation and friendship between Japan and Korea in the future. This was not just a personal note, for each Katô represented an elective base.

Shidzue's conversion to MRA was lifelong, outlasting the effectiveness and influence of that organization itself. In fact, MRA tenets seemed a natural religious progression from the first teachings of Christian humanism that she had joyfully received from Nitobe at the time of her marriage to the Baron Ishimoto, through her interest in Nichiren Buddhism in the late twenties, and her religious embrace of American democratic ideals in the thirties and forties. Her spiritual needs were great and her attitude toward doctrine eclectic. She tended to add on each new revelation rather than deserting the previous faith entirely.

The fact that her adherence to Buchman's principles endured speaks more to her idiosyncratic interpretation of religious values and her determination to act independently both personally and professionally than to MRA as an organization.

Family Planning for Japan and the World

In October 1952, after Japan had regained its sovereignty, the time seemed right once again to bring Margaret Sanger to Japan. With the help of Senator Katô this was easily accomplished. This time there was no visa problem, and no American Supreme Commander to prevent her entry. The weeklong event was a huge success. Sanger met with government officials and members of the family-planning movement; visited birth-control clinics; held press conferences; participated in radio round tables; and traveled around some of Tokyo's "slums," as Sanger referred to them, and to rural areas. (Katô called the same urban areas "working class" neighborhoods.)

On November 8, Sanger's final day in Japan, Katô and a JSP colleague took Sanger on a tour of Tokyo. They went about the streets in a campaign-style sound truck with loudspeakers. The two politicians gave Sanger a taste of their educational program, which borrowed from the traditional storytellers who traveled around Tokyo on bicycles with a box of story pictures and a drawer of candy. This method of attracting a crowd to listen to stories and look at illustrations had been first adapted successfully by the Communist Party. Now these two socialist women were trying to appropriate it for their own political message. They wanted to educate the populous about the democratic process, and would include a word or two about family planning as well. On this occasion the loudspeakers blared out, "Sanger is here! Sanger is here! Sanger says no more abortions." Each time the sound truck stopped a crowd gathered, the two women gave brief speeches, and then a man presented a puppet show illustrating good family practices including the use of birth control. This final day's events seemed a fitting, if exhausting, conclusion to Sanger's week.

Sanger's return to Japan had been a triumphant one for her and a productive one for Katô. It was obvious, however, that the positions of these two women had changed. Senator Katô had shown that she could exert more influence and provide more help for Sanger than the other way around. Now it was Sanger who approached her Japanese friend with great urgency, while Katô, whose public activities continued to grow, might have to keep her American friend waiting until she could find a window in her busy schedule.

Katô's national prominence and international exposure placed Tokyo in line for the 1955 conference of the **International Planned Parenthood Federation (IPPF)**. Shidzue and her associates in other birth-control organizations determined to form one federated alliance in time for this event. In March 1953, Katô, the husband and wife team Drs. Amano, Dr. Koya of the government's National Institute of Public Health, Dr. Majima and Mr. Mihara Shinichi met with Dr. C.J. Gamble of IPPF to discuss the 1955 conference. Over the next year Katô, Majima, Koya, and Professor Kitaoka Juitsu joined forces to inaugurate a new umbrella organization for family planning which would sponsor that event. The **Family Planning Federation of Japan (FPFJ)**, was born in April 1954.

At the same time the FPFJ was established, a new organization, the Japan Family Planning Association, was launched independently by Kunii Chôjirô. During the years to come Katô and Kunii cooperated so that these two organizations became complementary rather than competitive. In 1954 Kunii and Katô found a partial solution to their mutual problem of funding as together they carried out a project that provided their respective groups some financial stability. They sold condoms.

The two colleagues approached the Okamoto Rubber Company, Japan's largest condom maker, and asked to buy their product in large quantities at reduced prices, and then resell them for a small profit. Their successful negotiations assured that from that time to the present the sale of condoms would provide both organizations with a primary source of funding. From Kunii's perspective, Senator Katô, who was not only a famous member of the House of Councillors but a great pioneer in family planning, provided the influence through her illustrious name, while he provided the idea. Katô, on the other hand, remembers the event and the date slightly differently. "In 1956, Mr. Kunii and I put our heads together and came up with the ideal method for raising money for the JFPA while promoting its goal at the same time." Regardless of the ownership of the idea, the purchase of condoms at one-quarter of Okamoto's retail price, and their sale to couples at a one hundred percent mark-up meant funding for family planning and a convenient supply at reasonable prices for couples who wanted to use contraceptives. Additionally the new packaging and the brand name FP, family planning, went far to erase the stigma that associated condom use with protection against venereal disease.

The IPPF Conference of October 1955 was held as planned. Katô was named chair. She was afraid that the international guests would be critical of Japan's Eugenics Law with its apparent emphasis on abortion. Nervously she addressed this issue in her opening remarks. In an attempt to blunt criticism she stated, "Women in Japan think that abortion is not the answer for mothers suffering from the burden of unwanted children. The public demand that the scientific study of population and contraception should find a place in the public programs of the political parties." At this time no other country had such free access to legal abortion. Though Katô, herself, decried the implication that abortion should be seen as a birth-control method, she spent many hours explaining Japanese policy on abortion. She tried to emphasize the new government policies that substantially strengthened the case for birth-control alternatives to abortion. For example, she explained the rights of family-planning field workers to sell contraceptives, and the encouragement by the Ministry of Health and Welfare to offer family-planning counseling and free contraceptives to the poor.

The conference was considered by all to be a huge success. Though it had taken much of Katô's time and energy, she managed to set aside periods for other activities as well. These included publicizing birth control, seeking government support for research on a contraceptive pill, pressing for greater government funding to promote family-planning education, and lobbying for additional revisions to the Eugenics Law. The next year, 1956, Katô became chair of FPFJ and helped to organize the International Japan Planned Parenthood Committee, which then joined Sanger's IPPF organization. Shidzue at fifty-eight was as energetic as ever.

Continued Political Success

Katô found success in the House of Councillors as an advocate for women and children. She used her committee appointments well as she sought to obtain social and economic justice for families. For example, she made a significant imprint as a member of the Committee for Public Health and Welfare in spite of lacking the political clout that accrued to the party in power, the Liberal Democrats.

One success focused on nutrition for mothers and children, a long-standing crusade for Katô. As late as 1954 the Japanese people continued to experience basic nutritional deficiencies in their daily living. Although the Korean War had provided an economic windfall for the nation as a whole, individuals and families continued to be hard-pressed.

Shidzue learned as she traveled about talking with her constituents that farmers and urban workers in particular still struggled to provide for their families. On one such tour she met with dairy farmer wives in Chiba Prefecture and felt immediate sympathy for the harshness of their lives and the ceaseless nature of their work. Associating their economic problems with an inadequate vitamin intake for mothers and children nationwide, she thought of a mutually beneficial way to solve both urgent problems.

She suggested to her public health committee that a small investment in equipment would make it possible for local stores and kiosks in railway stations to provide low-temperature heating for milk and that this would be adequate to make the product safe for children. Easy access to relatively inexpensive milk would substantially increase a child's vitamin intake and would simultaneously provide a new outlet and increased profit for the dairy farmers, who were having difficulty convincing consumers of the benefits of drinking more milk. Some committee members opposed her program saying that Japanese culture would have to change for milk to become widely accepted, but in the end her measure was passed, providing one segment of the population with a better income and another with more nutrition.

The year 1956 was one of personal joy and political victory for Katô. In July she won reelection to the House of Councillors, receiving over 750,000 votes, almost twice the number of her first upper-house election, and placing first among the fifty people elected at this three-year interval. She was fifty-nine. Her campaign to secure her second six-year term had emphasized two issues: healthy family planning rather than abortion; and defense of the postwar constitution against revision. She did not want to see rearmament through modifications in the anti-military provisions of the constitution, for she felt women would be the losers in a Japan that jettisoned its pacifist stance. Her positions resonated with an enthusiastic public and her victory was glorious.

As a second-term senator with a strong national following Katô was able to advocate successfully in several new directions. She actively participated in writing and promoting the heavily debated anti-prostitution legislation that went into effect in 1957. Katô and other women in the JSP had worked off and on for such legislation since 1948. Each newly proposed bill reflected changes in their thinking as the Diet women debated among themselves over the issue of whether prostitutes should be treated as criminals or considered as women exploited by oppressive male pimps and customers. In the first bill, a prostitute, anyone who forced someone into prostitution, or anyone who ran a house of prostitution was classified as a criminal to be punished by imprisonment and a fine. By 1955, when a bill came very close to passing, the issue had become preventing prostitution without imposing criminal sanctions.

By the time the Prostitution Prevention Law went into effect, the goal was to "liberate" the women in paid sexual service while prohibiting houses of prostitution. There was also talk about rehabilitating prostitutes, but no funds were allocated. Unexpectedly, opposition to the legislation came from the prostitutes' union, the Tokyo Women Employees Alliance, and its two male JSP supporters, who felt that the law displaced women from their business and thus should include a compensation clause.

The figure of 30,000 yen a month was proposed, about what someone in middle management would make, but this was rejected.

The same year Katô inaugurated and led the Society for the Study of Women's Problems, a group which had branches in Tokyo, Osaka, Kobe, Nagano, Hiroshima, Yokohama, and Sendai and which published a monthly magazine and a newspaper. On the floor of the Diet she fought against conservative measures she felt would provide a setback to the democratic postwar gains achieved by women. As she wrote to America in January 1959, "We were busy trying our level best to fight for the cause of democracy against the present Japanese political power comprised of World War II culprits, which is now engaged in making laws which will eventually drag Japan into a reactionary pitfall." In this instance she was referring to the attempt of Prime Minister Kishi Nobusuke, who had been a minister in General Tôjô's cabinet, to pass a revision of the Police Duties Law. It was defeated in November 1958. This conflict with Kishi is of particular note because later that year Katô would see Kishi as a friend of family planning, and in 1960, she would support Prime Minister Kishi against the entire JSP on an issue of much graver consequences.

In each domestic issue that Katô pressed, in or out of the Diet, she tried to advocate for social justice for women and children, equal political rights for men and women, and political democracy that fairly distributed power in the service of these principles. Internationally she was imbued with a belief in social and economic justice for all peoples and special compensation for nationals who had suffered at the hand of Japan's imperial conquerors. Katô's early education in Christian humanism, her prewar experiences with the American and European liberalism, her observation of poverty and social inequality in Asia, and her selec-

tive understanding of the principles of "moral rearmament," all jumbled together in her mind to create a hazy
theory of international interaction based on economic justice, fair distribution of power, and human kindness and
love. Katô, ever the romantic, believed firmly in the good-
ness of people. But Katô was also a realist who saw an evil
side of humanity as well. She labeled this *communism*.

X

A Political Maverick

Senator Katô Shidzue and colleagues hold a press conference after attending a meeting on Asian Population growth and family planning, 1973. Ex-Prime Minister Kishi Nobusuke is to Katô's right. Courtesy Ashino Yuriko and The Family Planning Federation of Japan. Reprinted by permission.

Katô Shidzue believed her most significant accomplishments during the fifties and sixties were her achievements as an ad hoc international diplomat. In this role she was particularly influenced by her firm anti-communist stance and her strong support of America. To some extent this belief grew out of her support for MRA theology and her ideological conflicts with Japan Communist Party members. More important, however were her lifetime of international friendships and the open adulation she had received from officials during the American Occupation. In the end these ties were deeper and proved more binding than the weakening strands of Socialist Party control which demanded she follow party dictates.

Shidzue had seldom found the support or inclusion she had sought in the JSP, and she saw no reason to commit herself to fixed positions as formulated and pronounced by party leadership; she had specific international goals she would pursue whether or not the JSP or the Diet found them palatable. In the thirties she had found herself isolated and she had survived, while in the forties she had teamed with different groups as suited her objectives. Her independence had been tested in the most difficult of times and she was not afraid to stand alone. She had also experienced the elation and confirmation of public praise and believed that her leadership abilities had been judged satisfactory. She was therefore not afraid to make her own way in the years to come whether that meant alone or in association with a few others of like mind.

Apologizing to the Koreans

Shidzue was most proud of her endeavors on behalf of the Republic of Korea. During the fifties and sixties she pressed an independent, personal campaign directed at normalizing diplomatic relations with the South Korean government and improving personal contacts between the Japanese and South Korean peoples. This was not a popular cause in Japan, but it was one she felt deeply about. As she commented in 1978, "I had a chance to meet

Koreans in America after the war (1951). I extended my hand to shake in greeting but they would refuse to take it. I knew that they could speak Japanese but they preferred to converse in broken English. They told me bitter stories, many inside stories of suffering. They held bitter feelings against the Japanese. I thought it important for Japan to establish good feelings toward the Koreans. Japanese have found it easy to forget the damage which Japan did to the Korean nation but the Koreans have not forgotten." Her campaign for reconciliation, which was not officially sanctioned by either the government or her party, became significant because of the prestige of her elective office and her public popularity.

In April 1957, an MRA-sponsored conference for Asians was held in Baguio, the Philippines, and the organizers wanted a delegation from Japan to take part. This was not easy to arrange because there was no official treaty between the two countries and so travel visas required an extraordinary governmental agreement. In the end, newly elected Prime Minister Kishi Nobusuke facilitated the issuance of the necessary documents and a Japanese delegation of twenty, including Katô Shidzue, was formed. At the meeting, representatives from Korea, Taiwan, and Southeast Asia poured forth their hateful memories of the treatment they had received at the hands of the Japanese. It was a forceful exhibition of bitter acrimony that the Japanese delegation listened to with tears and accepted without contest.

The most dramatic outcome of this conference, as reported in the *Yomiuri Newspaper,* was exploratory talks between the Koreans and Japanese toward the establishment of diplomatic relations. This was nothing short of miraculous considering that this was not an officially sanctioned gathering. Moreover, since the occurrence of inflammatory remarks in 1953 at the Third Conference between government officials of Japan and the Republic of Korea, no further talks of reconciliation had been planned. On the other hand, Prime Minister Kishi had approved travel for the MRA delegation, and he had privately agreed to the request of one delegate, Hoshijima Nirô, to use this occasion to seek informally an end to the deadlock existing between Japan and **ROK**.

As a senator and a member of the Foreign Affairs Committee, Katô Shidzue was the highest elected official in the Japanese delegation, and as such figured prominently in newspaper accounts. Several days of discussions among Katô, Hoshijima, who was an influential House of Representatives member of the conservative Liberal-Democratic Party (LDP) and chairman of the Japanese-Korean Society, and Soon Yoong Sun, chairman of the Foreign Affairs Committee of the Korean National Assembly, determined that there might be a basis for reconciliation between their nations. Undoubtedly conciliatory feelings were aided by the fact that Katô and Hoshijima apologized to the Korean for Japanese oppression in Korea, and for the stubborn and negative attitudes of previous Japanese officials during earlier official talks. This is astonishing considering that even today Japanese government officials debate the controversial question of whether and how to apologize for its treatment and occupation of Asian nations during World War II. After the meeting ended, the Japanese returned home. A few days later the Korean delegation arrived in Tokyo en route home. Refusing to meet the Japanese anywhere but at MRA House, they were feted there by Shidzue, Kanjû and others who continued the positive discussions begun in Baguio.

After the Koreans returned home, Hoshijima and Katô Shidzue worked together to move the issue of Japan/Korea normalization forward in the Diet. Hoshijima agreed to discuss the progress made at the

MRA Conference with his friend Prime Minister Kishi. Shidzue promised to raise pertinent questions in the appropriate legislative manner of interpolation when Kishi appeared before the Foreign Affairs Committee on April 30, 1957. Katô admits that she spoke privately with Kishi before the committee exchange to lay out just what she intended to say.

According to the proceedings of that committee meeting, Katô asked her questions within a long summary monologue of what had taken place at Baguio. She included carefully phrased criticism of Japan's wartime oppression, and the subsequent good-faith actions of their associate the parliamentarian Mr. Yoong, in speeches before the Korean parliament. In this characteristic roundabout manner of Diet proceedings, she presented a full public account of her activities, including the apology for Japan's past actions, and asked the prime minister to begin a process of national reconciliation. The first action she requested was withdrawal of the Kubota Declaration, which claimed, among other things, that the Koreans should be appreciative of all that the colonial Japanese government had done for the Korean people. Katô then ended her statement, "I hope that in this Committee you, Mr. Prime Minister, will declare your sincerity in regard to this Kubota declaration. This statement has given the impression of superiority of the Japanese people to the Korean people. It expresses the attitude of the Japanese as a people, rather than a statement of one person, and as such I believe we should withdraw this declaration."

In the 1951 Peace Treaty Japan had officially accepted the existence and independence of the Republic of Korea (ROK–South Korea). At that time, however, many government officials and other citizens believed that Japan had no obligation to apologize for its past actions in Korea because Japan's rule had been both benevolent and beneficial, especially in areas of education, health, transportation, and agriculture. This attitude was evident in all three conferences between Japan and the ROK that occurred after the signing of the Peace Treaty. In 1953 Kubota Kanichiro, the chief Japanese delegate to the Third Conference on normalizing relations, had arrogantly stated that granting Korea independence before an official peace treaty was signed between the two nations was inappropriate; that the Allied Powers should be criticized for disposing of Japanese property before a peace treaty was negotiated; that the Japanese retained the right to make compensation claims for seized property; that the Japanese had not been bad rulers and in fact in several areas the Koreans had benefited substantially from colonial rule; and, finally, that the Cairo Declaration which accused the Japanese of enslaving the Koreans was an exaggeration. The Korean reaction to this tirade was to walk out of the meeting and refuse to return. The Katô/Hoshijima diplomacy resuscitated these talks.

At the April 1957 Foreign Affairs Committee meeting, Prime Minister Kishi, who had been primed for Katô's interpolation by Hoshijima and Katô herself, began his reply by saying that he agreed wholeheartedly with Mrs. Katô on every point as regards the normalizing of Japan–Korean relations. Then he added that in concurrence with Mrs. Katô, he believed that the most important issue was not the interpretation of the laws but the creation of trust and a spiritual understanding, and that the Japanese must take the initiative in this. He then unequivocally denounced the Kubota Declaration, and, although he insisted that it had not been an official statement but, rather, a private opinion, he officially withdrew the statement to prevent any misunderstanding.

Katô then tackled another stumbling block to reconciliation, financial claims which Japanese businesses and individuals had made for property lost when Japanese control over Korea was forfeited at the end of the war. In the exchange that followed, Katô implied that the Japanese government would have to provide the compensation these people deserved. Kishi did not so promise, but indicated such agreement might come to pass. Satisfied at the progress that had been made in the face of extremely difficult problems, Katô only asked that her government and its people "act with a humble attitude. It is so important to win the trust of the Korean people and I would like you, Mr. Prime Minister, to promise that the Government will do its best." The interpolation achieved the anticipated policy commitments Katô and Hoshijima desired. In a Joint Communiqué of December 31, 1957, Kishi officially withdrew the Kubota Declaration, and Japan/ROK treaty negotiations began once again. It took some time to achieve a full rapprochement, and not until February 17, 1965, under new administrations in both countries, did Japan's foreign minister make an official statement of regret to the ROK government and people for their unfortunate period under Japanese rule.

Since Katô was a member of the minority JSP and Kishi was the penultimate conservative leader of the LDP, the completely agreeable exchange in April 1957 on one of Japan's most sensitive issues of foreign policy would seem an anomaly. However, considering the growing economic significance of South Korea to Japanese postwar recovery, and the conciliatory policies within the JCP and JSP toward the communist leaders of North Korea, it is not so surprising that the LDP leadership saw advantages to normalizing relations with the ROK. The crux of the issue lies in placing a *South* in front of each mention of Korea in the exchange between Prime Minister Kishi and Senator Katô. This was not a matter of reconciliation with a people, but a matter of finding common economic and political ground that would solidify support for the South and further isolate and contain the North and its Japanese supporters on the left. Of equal importance in reviewing this most unusual LDP/JSP détente is the knowledge that Kishi was heavily influenced by, sympathized with, and soon became a part of MRA. This is why Hoshijima, also LDP and MRA, was able to work so closely with Kishi and why JSP Senator Katô and Kishi appeared to be involved in a carefully choreographed dance. A mutual respect for MRA, combined with Kishi's foreign policy concerns and Katô's determined effort to apologize to and reconcile with the Korean people, assured that these two apparent political opponents could reach concurrence. By this time Shidzue's actions had gone beyond those of an unbridled party member; she had become a political maverick.

A Public Conflict with the Socialist Party

There is another, even more striking, example of the closeness between Katô Shidzue and Prime Minister Kishi which emerged during the bitter debate and explosive demonstrations accompanying renegotiation of the **American-Japanese Security Treaty** in 1960. The animosity between the sides for and against this treaty was of such intensity that it created an indelible dividing line separating people ideologically, politically, and personally. Once again the conservative prime minister and the socialist senator found themselves unexpectedly in concert.

The treaty renewal had been approved by the U.S. Senate, and President Eisenhower was to make a triumphant trip to Tokyo in June 1960, by which time it was assumed that Kishi would have secured approval of the Japanese Diet. In fact, while the LDP majority did favor the treaty, the JSP and JCP were adamantly opposed. The left was firmly supported by many citizens who opposed the treaty's stipulation that the United States could station their military on Japanese soil free from any interference or control by Japan. People were further outraged that ships and planes arriving in Japan might carry nuclear weapons, and many cried foul over a possible collusion between the U.S. military and the Japanese government for a covert rearmament of the military under the guise of a Japanese self-defense force. Opposition to the treaty had the most vocal and demonstrative segments of the public on their side, and evidence further suggests that well over half of all of Japan's citizens opposed its renewal.

Disapproval of this LDP-sponsored legislation was formidable. Strikes were called by the most militant and largest union, and demonstrations were held by the radical **National Federation of Students.** Many students, laborers, and others snaked through the streets in long curving lines shouting their opposition to renewal. Worried about JSP/JCP tactics that might prolong the vote and cause difficulties for the Eisenhower visit, Kishi suddenly called an early morning session of the House of Representatives on May 20, while the Socialists were boycotting the Diet on a different issue. With this trickery he succeeded in getting the treaty approved.

Public response should have been as predictable as it was extreme. The strikes and demonstrations, the clashing with police, the general public outcry were without postwar precedent. On June 4 the labor union organized a three-hour strike of four million rail workers. On that same day the Socialists threatened to resign en masse, the students battled with police, and many anti-Eisenhower rallies were held. On June 10 students led by their union surrounded President Eisenhower's press secretary, who had just arrived at Haneda airport in advance of the president's visit. One group after another reacted forcefully in demonstration against Eisenhower's visit and treaty renewal. On the 15th, twelve thousand members and sympathizers of the National Federation of Students stormed the Diet; five hundred and ninety were injured and one woman was killed in the process. President Eisenhower declared that the rioting and demonstrations had been fomented by international communism. Two days later, accepting Kishi's advice, Eisenhower postponed his visit.

On June 19, while the JSP and JCP blocked any possibility of a House of Councillors' vote on the bill, the Security Treaty automatically became law in accordance with Diet rules. On June 24, pressed by the devastating disorder and strong public opposition to the treaty and to his methods of securing ratification, Kishi announced that he would soon resign, which he did within a month. This was an event of vastly significant proportions, and one about which the LDP and the JSP held diametrically opposed views.

One, and only one, member of the JSP stood with Kishi, and that was Senator Katô Shidzue. In a public declaration Shidzue defied her party, her husband, Kanjû, and her well-known cousins, Uncle Yûsuke's children, Tsurumi Kazuko and Tsurumi Shunsuke, who were outspoken leaders of the National Federation of Students. Once again Shidzue took an independent road based on her moral interpretation of events without regard to the political consequences for herself or those close to her. From the standpoint of her future within the party and her relationships with other socialists it was a debacle. According to her friends in MRA, it was an act of courage and righteousness. Whatever else, it was a milestone in her career and a turning point regarding future Diet influence.

For Shidzue, as for many who opposed the U.S./Japan Security Treaty, this confrontation, several years building, marked the end of the greater struggle for a democratic

Japan. Shidzue had dreamed in the late forties of a blood-less revolution that would bring about a socialist democracy guaranteeing equality for men and women, economic security for families, and justice for all. Her ideas were far more radical than what she had observed in America, but they were in line with what she believed she saw at SCAP, especially at CIE, during the early years of the American Occupation. Like so many other Japanese on the left, she had been dismayed and to some extent defeated by the so-called reverse course the Occupation officials seemed to institute as early as 1947. She was also angered by the institutional rigidity and exclusiveness of the JSP and the Diet. By 1950 she knew there would be no democratic revolution. At the same moment she saw a more serious threat to the simple survival of democracy in the rise of communism, especially in China. The Korean War confirmed this fear. Shidzue's support of Kishi and the treaty was the natural culmination of this train of thinking and political experience, just as opposition to this treaty was a natural progression for most others on the left, who likewise decried the death of a democratic revolution for Japan.

An Independent Road

From June 1960 on, Katô Shidzue distanced herself even further from the Socialist Party and from the left. This meant apparent disagreement with her husband, Kanjû, as well, although no personal conflict ensued. While Shidzue continued to sit as a JSP member in the House of Councillors, she had no party influence. In the public's eye she was still highly visible and popular, and she gained reelection twice more. Once again in 1962 she led the Socialist Party candidates, receiving over a million votes, placing second among the fifty candidates running at-large. In 1968 she dropped in number of votes and came in twenty-first out of the fifty, and in 1974, a good election for the Socialists, she came in fifty-eighth, one of only two out of twelve Socialist at-large candidates who failed to win election. She attributed her 1974 loss to the popular reformist campaign of Ichikawa Fusae, who drew from a similar constituency. Since the top fifty vote getters gained seats in the House of Councillors, she was not in direct competition with Ichikawa, but since each voter throughout the nation only had one vote, she felt that too many, choosing between her and another women's advocate of similar age and standing, cast their votes for Ichikawa. Katô was seventy-seven when she retired from elective politics.

Of the time spent as a senator after the 1960 debacle, Katô was most pleased with her work on the Industrial Pollution Committee and the Transportation Countermeasures Committee. Since House of Councillors committee chairs theoretically have substantially less power than their counterparts in the House of Representatives, they are often chosen from opposition parties. Katô chaired the transportation committee for two sessions in the late sixties and she chaired and then co-chaired the pollution committee once each during the early seventies, a period of substantial legislative activity in this area. It was JSP pressure that caused the calling of special sessions in 1970, and, in all, during these sessions, fourteen pollution laws were enacted. Katô felt that during this period she had made progress toward securing the public good. She supported LDP Prime Minister Tanaka's 1971 appointment of Ôishi Buichi, M.D., to be director general of the newly created Environment Agency, and the next year joined with him in publishing a book concerning conservation of nature, environmental pollution, and environmental health. The public valued her political and social positions, and listened when she spoke on environmental and conservation issues. It was this debate that generated women-led consumer movements of the seventies for better national health and welfare.

Katô's environmental interests grew out of her activism for the protection and humane treatment of animals, a cause that had received little attention in Japan. Beginning in 1958, Katô participated in **Japan's Society for the Prevention of Cruelty to Animals (JSPCA)**, presided over the organization from 1964 to 1977, and became chairman of the board. This small organization directs an ambitious program of education in animal protection and care, and the conservation and preservation of endangered species. Much energy has been expended on programs for children and teenagers, which include films, projects for "Be Kind to Animals" week, lectures and pamphlets, leaflets on care of pets, and special school programs. In addition the organization has frequently worked successfully at a local level to pressure individuals, businesses, and groups to cease activities harmful to animals, and it has lobbied, though not wholly successfully, for appropriate national protective legislation. Katô recalls that it took from 1965 to 1973 to pressure the Diet into passing one single animal protection law. At one point she combined her Foreign Affairs Committee assignment with her interest in animal preservation by working successfully for legislation that would support the exchange of wild birds between countries in an effort to preserve and protect wild life.

The most sensitive problems the organization has considered are those that affect the fishing industry. Passage of laws against net fishing or whaling is impossible. The organization did go on record in support of the International Whaling Commission's rulings, but at the same time they tried to show an understanding of the complex economic repercussions these would have for Japan's fishing industry. In an uphill battle Katô and her group supported the protection of dolphins caught by the indiscriminate practices of net fishermen, but such sensitive issues require cooperation. She believed "International understanding is a very important part of animal protection. In the United States a lot of dolphins are caught by the fishing industry but this (bad publicity) is counterbalanced by organizations which study dolphin behavior and which work to protect the dolphins." This is what the JSPCA is trying to do, but it is much too small, has a minuscule budget, and attracts too few sympathizers to bring about changes in Japan's fishing practices. According to Katô, the entire nation is blamed for animal losses caused by just one segment of society. Small victories are hard won. For example, in the early seventies the JSPCA lobbied successfully for protection of the Japanese antelope and preservation of its habitat. The primary attitude in Japan, she claimed, is that "human beings come first and so there is no time or energy to commit to the protection of animals."

Katô's primary recognition always came from her family-planning activism. This was the cornerstone of her activism from 1920 to the war years and was resumed with vigor after the end of World War II. She was vice-president of the Family Planning Federation of Japan from its inception and became its president in 1974, and she remained the president of record until her death in December 2001. In 1963 she helped establish the Western Pacific Regional Office for International Planned Parenthood in Tokyo, and in 1968 she helped inaugurate the **Japanese Organization for International Cooperation in Family Planning (JOICFP)** with her old LDP friend Kishi Nobusuke as chair. Katô joined the board of directors of this organiza-

1972. Katô Shidzue is awarded the First Order of Merit by the Emperor. In 1970 when her husband, Katô Kanjû was awarded the First Order of Merit, she received the Second Order of Merit. She was the first wife to be so honored. Courtesy of Katô Shidzue.

tion along with another longtime associate, Kunii Chôjirô. In 1984, after sixteen years on the board of directors of JOICFP, she was made vice-president. In 1974, to her great personal joy, the government recognized her work in family planning by awarding her the First Class Order of the Sacred Treasure, an honor presented to her by Emperor Hirohito.

Shidzue's beloved husband, Katô Kanjû, died on September 27, 1980, at the age of eighty-six. In her *Reminiscences,* written four years later, Shidzue told of his last illness and her grief at his passing. At that point she resolved to move on from mourning to action, and to live her life as fully as possible, continuing her political activities while drawing strength from meditation, a program of reading, and interacting with young people.

Epilogue

After 1960, Katô worked outside her party and outside other major organizations as a leader of small organizations or alone on a variety of issues. She followed her own commitments, experiencing small steps forward and occasional setbacks. This suited her post-Occupation expectation that incremental political change would result from valued individual contributions made for the general good of society. In none of these ventures did she receive the accolades of the early postwar years, but there is no doubt that her continued life of activism helped to advance the cause of public welfare.

Although the Family Planning Federation of Japan has provided forty years of education and practical support for women and families, it remains one of only three small planned-parenthood organizations. All are headquartered in Tokyo, and all have small staffs, limited budgets, and no government financing. Changing the Eugenics Law continues to be difficult, and physicians still monopolize the business of abortion. The government refused to legalize the contraceptive pill until pressed by women who, in 1999, objected to the government's supporting Viagra for men while continuing to oppose contraceptive pills for women. The government still recommends condoms over all other forms of contraception. In fact the government wishes couples would simply have more children, rather than practice birth control, to counter the declining birth rate. Birth-control education in Japan, though available, remains primitive, and contraception is still considered the responsibility of women. Sexual activity is still mythically expected to remain within the marriage bed and extramarital, homosexual, and premarital sex are purposely ignored. Recently, a modest program of sex education was introduced into the Ministry of Education controlled school curriculum, but it does not approach the requirements of family-planning advocates.

It is, however, in the arena of family planning that Katô Shidzue's name is known, through television programs, interviews, her own ten autobiographies, and articles in newspapers and journals. Her life story including extensive on-camera conversations with her daughter, Taki, was made into a documentary in 1997 to celebrate her 100th birthday. This film has been shown nationally and internationally and generated a congratulatory phone call and an audience with Empress Michiko wife of the **Heisei** Emperor, Akihito.

While activism for family planning has certainly been a major achievement in Shidzue's lifetime, perhaps this is not her most significant legacy in the struggle for women's freedom and independence in Japan. Rather it is a primary part of a broader feminist role most intensely played out in the thirties, forties, and fifties. Shidzue's determined and dangerous practice during the thirties of ignoring the growing oppression by the militarists and her continued courageous efforts for women's liberation must be recognized as an important, if small, counterweight to the successful government strategy of marginalizing liberal women. Management of these women was achieved through intimidation with "dangerous thoughts" laws and required membership in government-sponsored mass organizations in support of militarist policies. Shidzue's example provides a window on what might have been had democracy survived in prewar Japan. Moreover it records the echoes of opposition to militarism, which could still be heard in Japan until about 1942. Whatever name we give

Katô Shidzue and Taki enjoy a celebration of Shidzue's long life, 1995. Courtesy of Katô Shidzue.

to official Japan in the thirties—fascism, imperial fascism, or military authoritarianism—it was not a politically monolithic state; for, as Shidzue's activities illustrate, there were cracks and chinks in the power centers.

After the war it was in Shidzue's postwar crusades for women's equality under the new constitution and for improved economic livelihood for women and children that she displayed her greatest leadership. The election of women to the Diet was a political watershed, but most of those elected were not reelected and most female Diet members were marginalized. Shidzue, by contrast, was reelected with substantial majorities, and used her elective positions skillfully, both in the Diet itself and, more often, on the outside as a lever for political influence. She was one of the most successful women in public office during the late forties and early fifties, partly because of her national recognition and partly because of her acceptance by American Occupation officials. It must be expected, therefore, that some political decline followed the American "reverse course" of 1947–1948, when Occupation officials switched their support to the old guard on the political right and encouraged conservatives to solidify their power.

This "reverse course" also accounts, to a large extent, for the apparent lack of progress by newly liberated women in general. In the first year after the war it seemed that political and social gains for women would know no bounds, and women's organizations would enjoy a share of the nation's political power: women had entered the political equation and would have to be reckoned with. Shidzue's own successful campaigns, and even her failed ones, in those first few years certainly would have predicted this. For example, her triumphant fight for a changed civil code, and establishment of a Women's and Minors' Bureau, as well as the failed but politically sophisticated campaign against indiscriminate VD examinations, would all suggest the growing ability of women to use a variety of approaches to gain access to political and social power. Unfortunately the changed atmosphere at GHQ in the late forties, the cold war fears, and the strengthened position of male conservatives undercut women's movements. They could not, however, choke them off entirely.

Unstoppable by such conventional means of isolation, Shidzue continued to use her electoral success to move forward several causes. She was comfortable and welcomed in both national and international circles, and her public concerns stretched from the welfare of women and children to the welfare of citizens of nations brutalized by the wartime Japanese. She was moved to act, not to theorize, and women benefited from her successes and learned from her failures. She was dynamic, active, and able. When her democratic dream slipped away, she reinterpreted her social and political role. At that crucial juncture she fell into the arms of MRA and lost her aggressive social/democratic political drive while gaining personal solace and peace. It was, perhaps, an unfortunate meeting. On the other hand, given the continuous political hammerlock in which the conservative Liberal Democratic Party held Japan, it was difficult for anyone to press liberal or feminist principles. Perhaps Katô's quiet advocacy of a few causes through careful alliance with individuals of different political ideologies was appropriate to these politically constricted times.

Until her fall and surgery in 1998 she maintained contact with the public through the media, and with her professional associates through attendance at meetings. She spoke often on television, and wrote articles for a variety of popular magazines and newspapers as well as such erudite publications as *The Japan Economic Newspaper*. She also attended board meetings of the Family Planning Federation of Japan, adding her inspiration as president, and a word or two about the organization's plans for the future. Throughout the nineties Katô maintained her interest in current arguments on birth control and abortion and followed the trends in other causes she supported. She showed particular interest in the political education of young people, and lent her voice and energy to encouraging young women to seek careers in politics, though suggesting they do so outside the traditional parties. In recognition of her international stature, in July 1995, Vartan Gregorian, president of Brown University, presented Katô with an award for her contributions to "women's rights, human rights, and family planning." Her daughter Taki was present to accept for her mother.

When I visited Katô Shidzue in 1998 she was 101 and still alert and interested in the social and political issues of the day. Though confined to a wheelchair, she commented that while her legs would not follow her commands, her mind was still active. This was certainly borne out by our conversation. I learned that she intended to follow our long visit with a committee meeting with members of her family planning organization to choose a recipient for the Katô

Shidzue award. Her family: Ishimoto Arata, a retired university professor, and his wife, who live in Chiba; Sumiko, her physician husband, Ômori Nobuhisa and their son, Nobumasa, who, together, run the convalescent home where I met with Katô in Tokyo; and Taki and her architect husband, Kurokawa Masayuki, and their fourteen-year-old son, Sho, all remained close to Shidzue, providing daily companionship and support. Katô Kanjû's son, Nobuyuki, runs a publishing company, and he and his family also reside in Tokyo.

On March 2, 2001, Katô Shidzue celebrated her 104th birthday with a party of friends. During the last few years, she had remained alert and interested in political and social issues. She was still president of FPFJ and, since 1995, also president of JOICEF. In preparation for her death she had planned her funeral. She told her daughter, Taki, that it should be a happy event. "I wish people to feel cheerful for the death of a person beyond one hundred is very happy and peaceful."

Katô Shidzue died quietly in her sleep on December 22, 2001. The funeral was held on the 27th at the Katô family's Buddhist temple, Zuirin-ji, of the Nichiren sect, which is located in the old section of Tokyo called Yanaka. The priests read sutras to a large and distinguished gathering from Katô's worlds of family planning and politics and then, while children's songs played in the background, those gathered payed their respects by offering incense. Shidzue was buried in the temple cemetery next to her beloved husband, Kanjû.

A grand celebration of Katô's life was held at the Imperial Hotel on February 23, 2002. At the end of this event those present were given Shidzue's newly published final autobiography which focused on her years after the age of one hundred and was written with the help of her daughter, Taki. Katô Shidzue had lived in three centuries; her lifetime of accomplishments will continue to speak for her.

A Note on the Sources

The only biography of Katô Shidzue in English or Japanese is the one I wrote: *A New Woman of Japan: A Political Biography of Katô Shidzue,* by Helen M. Hopper (Westview Press, 1996). This much longer work has extensive footnoting and provides a listing of Japanese language sources. It was translated into Japanese under the title *Katô Shidzue, Living to One Hundred.* Katô wrote her first autobiography, *Facing Two Ways,* in 1935 in English and this was reprinted by Stanford University Press in 1983 with a foreword and afterword by Barbara Molony. After 1948, she wrote about ten autobiographies in Japanese, the most comprehensive of which were written before 1985. In addition, her 1937–1939 Diary was published in Japanese with notes and commentary by Funabashi Kuniko in 1988. Funabashi also published the first Japanese version of *Facing Two Ways* on its fiftieth anniversary, 1985. After turning one hundred Katô published two additional autobiographies. In addition to using these personal accounts, I have interviewed Katô extensively.

Archival research is often the most satisfying and exciting for a historian. Fortunately, there are several archives with primary sources about Katô in English covering her experiences from 1920 through the 1960s. Her correspondence with Margaret Sanger and Sanger's diaries of her trips to Japan and Katô's correspondence with others in the American birth-control movement can be found in the Sophia Smith Collection at Smith College in Northampton, Massachusetts, and the Library of Congress in Washington, D.C. Correspondence with Roger Baldwin is in Princeton University Libraries, and audiotapes of Baldwin in the Library of Congress include his comments on his trip to Japan. The U.S. Archives, National Records Center, College Park, Maryland, houses the material from the American Occupation of Japan and is filled with documents, notes, comments, letters, and so forth that refer to Katô and events in which she participated. Although much of this archive has now been microfilmed, working with the loose papers in boxes in all of their disorder is both easier and more rewarding. Small bits of paper, out of order, which have slipped deep into folders often provide unexpected information. Unfortunately the Family Planning Federation of Japan has not archived its material, but gems of information have been passed along to me by one of its administrators, Ashino Yuriko. The Japanese Organization of International Cooperation in Family Planning in Tokyo has produced Katô's only book on family planning, *A Fight for Women's Happiness* (1985), written in English.

Several general texts on modern Japan would give a quick overview of politics, labor, women, war, and so forth. These would include: Marius B. Jansen, *The Making of Modern Japan* (Harvard University Press, 2000); Kenneth B. Pyle, *The Making of Modern Japan*, 2nd ed. (D. C. Heath and Co., 1996); Peter Duus, *Modern Japan*, 2nd ed. (Houghton Mifflin Co., 1998); Mikiso Hane, *Modern Japan: A Historical Survey* (Westview Press, 1986); and for just postwar Japan, Mikiso Hane, *Eastern Phoenix: Japan Since 1945* (Westview Press, 1996); and Gary D. Allinson, *Japan's Postwar History* (Cornell, 1997); John Halliday, *A Political History of Japanese Capitalism* (Monthly Review Press, 1975). For general texts that focus on twentieth-century Japan in an international context there are *Modern Japan: The American Nexus,* by John Hunter Boyle (Harcourt Brace Jovanovich, 1993); *Japan & the Wider World,* by Akira Iriya (Longman, 1997); *Japan and the World Since 1868,* by Michael A. Barnhart (Edward Arnold, 1995); and *Clash: U.S.–Japanese Relations Throughout History* by Walter LaFeber (W.W. Norton, 1997). Also one could look at *Peasants, Rebels, and Outcasts: The Underside of Modern Japan,* by Mikiso Hane (Pantheon, 1982), particularly for social history of peasant women, prostitutes, and coal miners. *Showa: The Japan of Hirohito,* ed. by Carol Gluck and Stephen R. Graubard (W.W. Norton, 1992), has a collection of essays by Americans and Japanese covering the period of Hirohito's ascension to the throne in the 1920s to his death in 1989. Andrew Gordon has edited a collection of political, social, and intellectual essays on topics from the war's end, *Postwar Japan as History* (University of California Press, 1993), which would be essential to understanding this fifty-year period.

There are many worthwhile secondary sources in English that give background to events mentioned in the book. The following is just a taste of what is available. The most comprehensive book on the Occupation Period is John Dower's Pulitzer–prize-winning work *Embracing Defeat: Japan in the Wake of World War II* (W.W. Norton, 1999); equally important is the Pulitzer–prize-winning work, *Hirohito and the Making of Modern Japan,* by Herbert P. Bix (HarperCollins, 2000). A useful and readable single volume on the war is *Japan's War,* by the journalist Edwin Hoyt (McGraw-Hill, 1986). For a Japanese version of events leading to war, the war itself, and its aftermath, see *The Age of Hirohito: In Search of Modern Japan,* by Daikichi Irokawa (The Free Press, 1995). *Japan at War: An Oral History,* by Haruko Taya

Cook and Theodore F. Cook (The New Press, 1992), gives first-person vignettes of Japanese citizens from the 1920s through the end of the war. Thomas R. H. Havens, *Valley of Darkness: The Japanese People and World War Two* (University Press of America, 1986) is a treasure trove of detail about life in Japan during the war and is especially strong on women and children.

Social history from the turn of the twentieth century until the forties can be found in the first-person stories drawn together by Dr. Junichi Saga in *Memories of Silk and Straw: A Self-Portrait of Small-Town Japan* (Kodansha, 1987). Donald T. Roden has written a detailed work on education before the war, *Schooldays in Imperial Japan: A Study in the Culture of a Student Elite* (University of California Press, 1980). For material on political crimes, prisons, sentencing, and the working of the interwar justice system see Richard H. Mitchell, *Janus-Faced Justice, Political Criminals in Imperial Japan* (University of Hawaii Press, 1992); and for details on "thought crimes" and the Peace Preservation Law, Mitchell has written *Thought Control in Prewar Japan* (Cornell University Press, 1976). *Japanese Police State: Tokkô in Interwar Japan,* by Elise Tipton (University of Hawaii, 1990), adds yet more to our understanding of the prewar justice system as embodied in the special higher police.

Some of the most useful materials on women's history are contained in edited volumes with a variety of time periods and topics. Two that are often used as classroom texts are (prewar) Gail Lee Bernstein, ed., *Recreating Japanese Women, 1600–1945* (University of California Press, 1991) and (postwar) *Re-Imaging Japanese Women,* Anne E. Imamura, ed. (University of California Press, 1996). Japanese women have contributed a collection of essays on contemporary women's lives, *Japanese Women: New Feminist Perspectives on the Past, Present, and Future,*

Kumiko Fujimura-Fanselow and Atsuko Kameda, eds. (Feminist Press, 1995). Sheldon Garon's book, *Molding Japanese Minds: The State in Everyday Life* (Princeton University Press, 1997), has chapters on prewar women's groups and on prostitution and welfare, and postwar chapters on moral issues and the feminization of social management. There has been only one modern chronological history of Japanese women, *The Hidden Sun: Women of Modern Japan,* by Dorothy Robins-Mowry (Westview Press, 1983); it is a detailed catalogue of specific women and their contributions to modern Japanese political and social history. *Flowers in Salt: The Beginnings of Feminist Consciousness in Modern Japan,* by Sharon L. Sievers (Stanford University Press, 1983) takes women's history from 1868–1918. Kazuko Smith has translated *Makiko's Diary, A Merchant wife in 1910 Kyoto* (Stanford University Press, 1995), which adds greatly to our understanding of Meiji women. Mikiso Hane's *Reflections on the Way to the Gallows: Rebel Women in Prewar Japan* (University of California Press, 1988) gives biographies of nine radical women and two groups, often letting the women speak for themselves during the period of the late nineteenth century through the 1930s. The Keio University Professor of Psychology Sumiko Iwao has written a contemporary look at women, *The Japanese Woman: Traditional Image & Changing Reality* (The Free Press, 1993). Several American historians are currently writing biographies of Japanese women who paralleled Katô in political and social causes, including Barbara Molony, who is working on Ichikawa Fusae, and Sally Hastings, who is writing on four postwar Diet women.

A reading of women's history is not complete without some acquaintance with literature. Fortunately, translations of women's novels and short stories have gained favor and many are now available in books and in journals. Two collections I have often used in class are *To Live and To Write,* ed. by Yukiko Tanaka (The Seal Press, 1987), which is particularly revealing of women in the 1920s and 1930s, and *Japanese Women Writers,* trans. and ed. by Kyoko Iriye Selden and Noriko Mizuta Lippet (M. E. Sharpe, 1991), which includes stories written from the thirties through the eighties.

On family planning and birth control one can look at Samuel Coleman's *Family Planning in Japanese Society: Traditional Birth Control in a Modern Urban Culture* (Princeton University Press, 1991). This is the most accessible work; for additional writings one would need to consult specialized journals. Accessible in some libraries would be the very useful *U.S.–Japan Women's Journal: A Journal for the International Exchange of Gender Studies,* produced jointly by Josei University in Japan and Purdue University in the United States. It often has material on family planning as well as a wide array of other women's topics. For the American side I find Ellen Chesler's *Woman of Valor: Margaret Sanger and the Birth Control Movement in America* the most useful. There are many books both by Sanger and about her, but none of them, certainly not her own autobiographies, manages to portray accurately Katô Shidzue or Japan.

Most of the works mentioned are still in print and available in soft-cover editions. I have used most of them at one time or another in college courses and find them helpful for teaching and readable by undergraduates.

Glossary

ACLU: American Civil Liberties Union, headed by Roger Baldwin.

Allied Occupation: official title of occupation to be administered by all victorious allies of WWII.

American Occupation: informal and more accurate title for administration of occupation.

American-Japanese Security Treaty: provides for U.S. military bases in Japan, first negotiated after Peace Treaty signed in 1952, renegotiated at later dates, still in force.

B.C.: birth control.

BCJ: Broadcasting Corporation of Japan—later called by Japanese letters NHK (Nihon Hôsô Kyôkai).

Birth Control League of Japan (1931): early organization founded by Katô Shidzue.

Bismarck's state socialism: Chancellor (1871–1890) Otto von Bismarck's conservative measures to provide welfare for Germans while maintaining absolute state control.

Black market: illegal markets that sold scarce goods at higher than official prices.

Bolshevik: extreme radical; from party that took control of Russia in November 1917.

Bushidô: rituals performed by *samurai* class in premodern Japan; way of the warrior.

China Incident: Japan's euphemistic description of their war with China (1937–1945).

Christian humanism: philosophy drawn from both Christian ethics and values centered on humankind.

CIE: Civil Information and Education—division of the American Occupation's power structure.

Cold War: standoff between the United States and U.S.S.R. and between the Western democracies and Eastern communist block; later included U.S. followers in Asia versus Communist Asia.

Comfort the troops: cultural and political celebrities who were sent by the Japanese government to cheer the soldiers fighting in China; not to be confused with "comfort women" who were women forced to become prostitutes to service Japan's army.

Dangerous thoughts: catch-all phrase for anything the government determined threatened the state or emperor; definition constantly changing.

Diet: Japanese parliament both before and after the war, composed of upper and lower houses.

Eugenics, Eugenics Law: breeding for the improvement of the nation or race; term applied to Japan's law covering birth-control measures and abortion rights.

Family register: official record of all pertinent data for families, usually located in ancestral home and containing statistics for marriages, births, deaths, illnesses, etc.

Fascism, fascist, fascistic: terms often applied to Japan during the 1930s and 1940s, usually inaccurately, often simply used as a label of condemnation; refers to Japan's militarist and imperialist policies, cannot equate with wartime Germany or Italy.

February 26 Incident: attempted but failed military coup by young right-wing army officers in 1937.

Feudal, feudalistic: refers to oppressive laws and behaviors of those (for example, men) who oppress others (especially women)—often simply used to condemn behaviors.

FPFJ: Family Planning Federation of Japan; Katô Shidzue was president until death in December 2001.

Friends of the Government Party: *Seiyûkai*—conservative prewar political party.

Geisha: high-class entertainer who is sometimes a prostitute.

GHQ: General Douglas MacArthur's General Headquarters, used interchangeably with SCAP.

Good wife, wise mother: saying used to emphasize women's subservient role in society.

Grassroots democracy: political action at the community level using basic constitutional freedoms as a guide.

Greater Japan Defense Women's Association: *Dai nihon rengô fujinkai*—prewar women's group of rural and lower-class urban women, dominated by the army and the Ministry of Defense and run by men.

Haori: Japanese traditional-style jacket to wear over a kimono.

Heisei: name of current era (1989–) and posthumous name of current Emperor Akihito.

House of Councillors: upper house of the legislature (Diet); members are senators.

House of Peers: prewar upper house of the legislature (Diet).

ILO: International Labor Organization, formed in Versailles after World War I.

Imperial Household Agency: administers all imperial family matters, very secretive.

Imperial Japan: term for the Japanese state before Japan was defeated in World War II.

IPPF: International Planned Parenthood Association—founded by Margaret Sanger.

JCP Japan Communist Party, made illegal prewar, legalized in 1945.

JOICFP: Japan Organization for International Cooperation in Family Planning.

JSP: Japan Socialist Party (today called Democratic Socialist Party), left-wing party.

JSPCA: Japan Society for the Prevention of Cruelty to Animals.

Kokutai: term used to signify the national entity, or polity headed by emperor; has sacred overtones.

Kwantung Army: Japanese Army in Manchuria/Manchukuo and China.

LDP: Liberal Democratic Party, postwar conservative party, formed in 1955 from right-wing Liberal and Democratic parties.

League of Nations: international organization founded after World War I to which Japan belonged but which the United States did not join; President Woodrow Wilson's idea.

Lower House: House of Representatives in the parliament (Diet).

Manchukuo/Manchuria: northern area of China administered and economically exploited by the Japanese but never officially incorporated as a colony.

Meiji: posthumous name for the Emperor Meiji and for his reign from 1868–1912.

Meiji Civil Code of 1898: set of laws that included family regulations which subordinated women to men, wives to husbands, and made husbands household heads.

Misô **soup:** bean-paste soup, a staple food.

MRA: Moral Re-Armament, anti-communist, quasi-religious organization.

National Federation of Students: *zengakuren*—powerful left-wing association of student organizations.

Neighborhood association: *tonarigumi,* group of ten neighborhood families who distributed rationed items during war and assured local patriotism.

New woman: 1920s women with Western attitudes and independent aspirations.

Patriotic Women's Association: *Aikoku fujinkai*—prewar women's group sponsored by the Home Ministry, included middle- and upper-class women, headed by men.

Peace Preservation Law of 1925: upgrading of previous laws that protected the state against activities deemed to be in opposition to the empire.

Pessary: rubber birth-control device, invented in the 1850s, similar to modern vaginal diaphragm.

Popular front: proposed international unification of communist and socialist parties in opposition to German and Italian fascism of the thirties.

Popular Government Party: *Minseitô*—more liberal of two largest prewar parties.

Proletarian Party: *Nihon musantô,* prewar left-wing socialist party founded by Katô Kanjû.

Purge: U.S. Occupation's elimination of military, political, and economic wartime leaders from the rolls of voters, bureaucratic positions, or candidates for public office.

Red purge: firing of workers, teachers, journalists, etc., from jobs on the grounds that they were communists or communist sympathizers (1949–1950).

Reverse course: Japanese label given to occupation after about 1947, when it appeared that the Americans began favoring the political right wing.

ROK: Republic of Korea (South Korea).

Samurai: warrior class before 1600, upper class during Tokugawa Period (1600–1867).

SCAP: Supreme Command(er) of the Allied Powers—both General MacArthur and the occupation in general.

Shintô: native religion of Japan—way of the gods.

Shogun: military ruler of Japan during Tokugawa Period (1600–1867).

Shôwa: era and reign name for Hirohito, who was emperor between 1926–1989.

Special higher police: "thought police," national police who enforced the Peace Preservation Laws and were much feared by the public.

Taishô: Posthumous name of the Emperor Taishô and his era (1912–1926).

Tatami **mats:** reed mats, about three feet by six feet, which are used on the floors of homes.

Tenkô: to turn over, to publicly express a change of heart and take up the causes of Imperial Japan, applied particularly to arrested left-wing thinkers and writers.

Tokugawa: name of the clan that provided the shogun who ruled Japan 1600–1857.

Tonarigumi: see Neighborhood association.

Water trades: *mizu-shôbai*—women's work in entertainment, prostitution, bars, or geisha houses.

Women's Birth Control League of Japan (1933): Katô Shidzue's second prewar birth-control organization.

Women's Suffrage League: organization founded in 1924 by women seeking political rights, including the vote and the right to run for political office.

Yoshiwara: famed district of Tokyo, set aside for legal, goverment-licensed prostitution.

Index